History of Cambridge, United Kingdom

State of Advancement, Economy and Environment

Author
David Mills.

SONITTEC PUBLISHING. All rights reserved. No part of this publication may be reproduced, distributed, or transmitted in any form or by any means, including photocopying, recording, or other electronic or mechanical methods, without the prior written permission of the publisher, except in the case of brief quotations embodied in critical reviews and certain other noncommercial uses permitted by copyright law. For permission requests, write to the publisher, addressed "Attention: Permissions Coordinator," at the address below.

Copyright © 2019 Sonittec Publishing
All Rights Reserved

First Printed: 2019.

Publisher:
SONITTEC LTD
College House, 2nd Floor
17 King Edwards Road,
Ruislip
London
HA4 7AE

Table of Content

- **SUMMARY** 1
- **THE CITY OF CAMBRIDGE, UNITED KINGDOM** 4
- **MIDDLE AGE** 8
- **MODERN HISTORY** 37
- **CONSTITUTIONAL HISTORY** 70
  - Town Records 70
  - The Earls and the Third Penny 73
  - Town Charters 75
  - Arms, Seal and Regalia 80
  - Firma Burgi 83
  - Bailiffs 85
  - Mayors and Aldermen 89
  - Common Council 104
  - Freemen 108
  - Town Assembly or Common Hall 115
  - Town Courts 119
  - Justices of the Peace 127
  - Town Clerk 130
  - Coroners 134
  - Recorder 135
  - High Steward 138
  - Town Waits 140
  - Treasurers and Town Revenues 142
- **ECONOMIC HISTORY** 158
  - Medieval Trade and Industry 158
  - Fairs 169
  - Jews 177
  - Banks 180
  - Modern Economic Development 183
- **TOWN AND GOWN** 192
  - Police 193
  - Morals 197
  - Theatres 198
  - Health 203
  - Jurisdiction 204
  - Trade 207
- **PUBLIC HEALTH** 216
- **GROWTH OF THE CITY** 234

History of Cambridge, United Kingdom

Summary

The world is a book and those who do not travel read only one page.

History Contributes to Moral Understanding

History is power of union, culture, development, creation. History. History also provides a terrain for moral contemplation. Studying the stories of individuals, Nation, City and situations in the past allows a student of history to test his or her own moral sense, to hone it against some of the real complexities individuals have faced in difficult settings. People who have weathered adversity not just in some work of fiction, but in real, historical circumstances can provide inspiration. "History teaching by example" is one phrase that describes this use of a study of the past a study not only of certifiable heroes, the great men and women of history who successfully worked through moral dilemmas, but also of more ordinary people who provide lessons in courage, diligence, or constructive protest

It is indeed very unfortunate that some people feel traveling is a sheer waste of time, energy and money. Some also find traveling an extremely boring activity. Nevertheless, a good majority of people across the world prefer traveling, rather than staying inside the confined spaces of their homes. They love to explore new places, meet new people, learn new History of places and things, and see things that they would not find in their homelands. It is this very popular attitude that has made tourism, one of the most profitable, commercial sectors in the world.

People travel for various reasons. Some travel for work, others for fun, and some for finding mental peace. Though every person may have his/her own reason to go on a journey, it is essential to note that traveling, in itself, has some inherent advantages. For one, for some days getting away from everyday routine is a pleasant change. It not only refreshes one's body, but also mind and soul. Traveling to a distant place and doing exciting things that are not thought of otherwise, can rejuvenate a person, who then returns home, ready to take on new and more difficult challenges in life and work. It makes a person forget his worries, problems, frustrations, and fears, albeit for some time. It gives him a chance to think wisely and constructively. Traveling also helps to heal; it can mend a broken heart.

For many people, traveling is a way to attain knowledge, and perhaps, a quest to find answers to their questions. For this, many people prefer to go to faraway and isolated places. For believers, it is a search for God and to gain higher knowledge; for others, it is a search for inner peace. They might or might not find what they are looking for, but such an experience certainly enriches their lives

David Mills

The City of Cambridge, United Kingdom

Cambridge, the county town, and since 1951 a city, owes its position to the crossing of two natural lines of communication. The Cam, constituting a river route from south-west to north-east, was a main artery for traffic through the Fenland until the railway period; as the Recorder of Cambridge said in his speech to James I in 1615, 'This river, with navigation to the sea, is the life of traffic to this town and county.' It was the chalk and gravel ridge that determined the line of the road which continued the Worsted Street to Huntingdon. Known in the Middle Ages as Stoneway or Huntingdon Way, it crossed the river by 'the one bridge in England which gives name to a county'. Roads from St. Neots and Ely join the Huntingdon Road west of the bridge, and to the east roads from Newmarket, Bishop's Stortford, Ware, and Baldock converge on the city.

To the end of the 18th century the built-up area of Cambridge was concentrated round the castle site north-west of the bridge and the market-place south-east of it, roughly 1 mile long and ½ mile broad, surrounded by the town fields which stretched east and west for 3½ miles. Outlying settlements at Barnwell downstream and Newnham upstream were only absorbed by the expansion of the 19th century which, beginning along the Newmarket Road, extended the built-up areas southwards and northwards both sides of the river until the houses of Cambridge in 1951 extended 2½ miles southeast of the bridge and a mile to the north. In 1912 and 1935 the Borough boundaries were successively extended to include the whole of Chesterton and Cherry Hinton and parts of Impington and Milton, Fen Ditton, Great Shelford, Trumpington, and Grantchester. The remains of the medieval town fields are to be seen south-west of the Huntingdon Road and in the various 'pieces' and college playing fields. 'Medieval Cambridge is largely separated from the expanding Cambridge of today by a ring of open land formed by the Commons and the Backs.'

It was counted a day's journey from London to Cambridge in the 14th century, and in 1702 a coach took 15 hours. The first coach ran from Cambridge to London in 1653. From 1663 onwards turnpike trusts were improving communications, and between 1724 and 1797 a series of Acts for improving the road between Cambridge and London and other main roads was passed. By the second half of the century there was a daily coach service to London, with others running to

Birmingham, Norwich, Yarmouth, and all the chief centres of East Anglia. In 1837 ten different coaches left Cambridge for London every week day, and two for Oxford. The last stage coach left Cambridge in 1849. The first milestones in England since the Roman occupation were erected along the London road by Trinity Hall in 1729 and bore the college arms; the first, at Trumpington Ford, was over 12 ft. high. There was also a regular boat service from 1774 and proposals for a canal to link the Cam with the Thames by way of the Stort were being mooted, but they were opposed both by the Corporation and the conservators of the Cam. The suggestion of a railway was also resisted from 1825 to 1842, when the first Act was passed. Not until 1845 was the line from London to Norwich opened by the Great Eastern, and then, owing to University influence, the station was placed over a mile from the centre of the town, and a subsequent project for a line over Coe Fen with a station on Sheeps Green or Midsummer Common was abandoned as likely to spoil the beauties of the place. The Great Northern, Midland, and London and North Western lines, opened in 1847, 1851, and 1862, linked Cambridge with most of the surrounding country.

The first mention of a post office operating in Cambridge was in 1672, when the postmaster asked to be exempted from quartering militia. The present building, which also houses the automatic telephone exchange, is situated in St. Andrews Street and was opened in 1934, about 150 yards from the site of the previous office at the corner of Petty Cury. A telegraph service was first provided by the Post Office in 1870, and the telephone service instituted by the National Telephone Company in 1892 was taken over in 1912.

Middle Age

The same physical features that make the site of Cambridge a natural centre for trade give it strategic significance, and the camp on Castle Hill, guarding the river crossing of the road from the Roman base at Colchester to Godmanchester on Ermine Street, may well have been erected in the early days of the Claudian conquest. If a RomanoBritish settlement existed on the site, it was insignificant in the 7th century when Bede tells of the 'little ruined city called Grantchester' where the monks of Ely found a stone coffin to enshrine the bones of Etheldreda. Archaeological discoveries, however, indicate the existence of pagan Saxon settlements on both sides of the river, and evidence as to ancient defensive ditches serving as bridge-heads is held to point to a time when Cambridge was on the frontier between East Anglian and Middle Anglian territory. It has been suggested that the replacing of a ford by a bridge may correspond to a revival of traffic and peace under Mercian ascendancy. It is noteworthy that only the hundreds west of the Granta those in Mercian territory were later responsible, by paying pontage, for the upkeep of the bridge.

When Cambridge is next mentioned, it is again as a strategically significant centre. The transition from Danish raids to Danish colonization is marked by the establishment of Cambridge as a military and administrative centre. The occupation by three Danish kings in 875 was temporary, but the 'army that belonged to Cambridge' and chose Edward as their lord in 921 must have been settled in the surrounding countryside, and it is probable that the organization of the shire after the English reconquest endorsed the arrangements of the Danish occupation. Thus Cambridge became the county town that it has been ever since, the centre both of local trade and of local government, surrounded by the fourteen rural hundreds south of the Isle of Ely, and itself the fifteenth. Traces of the Danish phase of its history may be seen in terminations such as 'wong' and 'holm', in the existence in the 12th century of names like Ketel and Turketel among the townsmen; possibly in the dedication of St. Clement's church; in the institution of the 24 lawmen and the classification with Norwich, Thetford, and Ipswich mentioned by the *Liber Eliensis*, and most significantly, in the story of the merchants from Ireland who brought cloaks for sale to Cambridge, and were probably Danes from Wexford and Dublin. The Ely chronicler describes a number of courts held at Cambridge in the century before the Norman Conquest, some undoubtedly shire moots, held near the 'Maiden Borough', others 'pleas of the townsmen'. He also mentions country dwellers who held land in the town, a feature of Cambridge life which persisted throughout the Middle Ages and indeed to modern times, and is further illustrated by the Guild of Cambridge thanes; a sort of country club whose rules provide for the religious, the convivial and the criminal liabilities of the Cambridgeshire aristocracy who made up its membership. Further evidence of the economic standing of Cambridge is afforded by the existence of a mint there from 975 onwards. Coins of five pre-Conquest kings are extant. The later Saxon tower of St. Bene't's church indicates that in addition to the dwellings west of the river served by the 10th-century church on Castle Hill, there was a prosperous settlement to the east, which may, if we can argue from archaeological evidence, have extended to the line of the town ditch. It seems highly probable that this ancient monument was originally designed rather as a customs barrier than as a defensive work and that the Barnwell gate and Trumpington gate of the 13th century were first and foremost toll gates.

The Domesday account of the Borough is brief and very possibly incomplete, but has significant features. Like Chester, York, Stamford, and Lincoln, Cambridge has lawmen; like Norwich, Thetford, Colchester, and Oxford and some others, it is assessed as a hundred; and it is one of the very few whose internal divisions are mentioned. Under the last Saxon sheriff its lawmen had paid a heriot, which the Norman sheriff Picot had increased eightfold, further adding a horse and armour. Taken in conjunction with the guild of thegns this suggests a thegnly status comparable with that of the burgesses of Hereford and Chester and the *burh witan* of Devonshire and recalling the traditional acquisition of thegn right by North Sea trade. Hugh Domesman, Prior of Barnwell 1155–75, who gave to the priory the extensive property that he inherited from his father, may have been the descendant of a Cambridge lawman.

Ten wards are assigned to Cambridge in Domesday Book, but only nine are described. Of the various theories produced to account for this Mr. Salzman's suggestion that the omission is accidental seems the most plausible. The total of 373 burgages in 1066 would thus be incomplete, and the fact that 27 houses had been destroyed and that 49 house plots were vacant makes it impossible to estimate the number of burgesses in 1086 with any assurance. Mr. Stephenson classes it with Colchester, Stamford, and Leicester, giving it the thirteenth place among English boroughs in 1066 and the fourteenth in 1086. As regards its value to the Crown, if the Domesday account is complete, Cambridge would rank still lower, coming after Northampton, Shrewsbury, and Huntingdon. It has been suggested, however, that some items have dropped out. Huntingdon's total is made up of landgavel, farm of the borough, mint dues, and mill dues, the earl taking his third penny of all of them. The Cambridge payments are £7 3*s*. 6*d*. in landgavel; £7 in 'customs' with £9 from the mills. In the 12th century the third penny of the Borough, payable in

Cambridge as in Huntingdon to the earls of Huntingdon, was £10 in Cambridge as it was in Huntingdon. It seems probable, then, that something has dropped out of the Domesday account of the town revenues of Cambridge. In the 12th century its 'ancient farm' was £40, and by 1189 an increment of £20 was added. Its ranking for the payment of *dona* or aids in 1130 and 1156 is also thirteenth, though it pays £12 where Huntingdon pays £8. But to describe Cambridge in 1086 as 'little more than an overgrown village' hardly does justice to the facts. It may have been 'cast in an agrarian mould'; but, as Maitland also says, 'it paid ten times what the ordinary Cambridgeshire village would pay.'

The tenants in chief holding burgages in 1086 were Count Alan, the first landholder in the county, lord of what was to be called the Honor of Richmond; the Count of Mortain, whose Cambridge holdings seem to have come into the hands of the earls of Leicester; and the Abbot of Ely. At last we have proof positive of an omission in the survey; the *Inquisitio Eliensis* records the abbot's holdings as ten messuages, two houses, a mill, a church, three gardens, and a croft, but Domesday mentions nothing but the mill, in connexion with Picot's new rival mills. Besides the magnates, three small county tenants had burgages; Ralph de Bans, a tenant of Picot's and Count Alan's in Pampisford, Barrington, Kingston, and Rampton, and one of the jurors of Wetherly hundred, Erchengar of Toft and Comberton, the King's serjeant baker, and Roger of Childerley, a man of the Bishop of Lincoln and a juror of Chesterton hundred. None of the burgages with external lords named by Domesday paid anything, and the fiscal privileges of Ely leave no doubt that the abbot's burgages were equally exempt.

The liveliest impression made by the Domesday account of the town is of the burgesses' resentment of their treatment by Picot, sheriff of Cambridgeshire 1070–92, the villain of the Ely and Rochester chroniclers and the 'deservedly honoured' hero of the Barnwell book. His exaction of ploughing and carting services from the townsmen reflects the wide extent of his holdings in the shire no less than the 'agrarian frame' of the Borough. The three new mills that he erected encroached on their building space and pasture as well as on the custom of the lords of other mills and one had been destroyed before 1086 in obedience to royal orders.

The importance of Cambridge in political history is regional rather than national. Twice in the Middle Ages and once in modern times it served as a military base; in the 11th and 13th centuries for operations against the island stronghold of Ely, the last home of defeated causes, in the 17th century as guarding the line of communications between East Anglia and the north and as constituting the centre of organization for that prosperous and parliamentarian countryside. But no pitched battle took place there, no councils of importance were held there, and only one Parliament met there. The very fact that

Cambridge was off the route of marching armies made it a natural centre in economic and cultural affairs; Sturbridge Fair and the University testify to its twofold advantage of accessibility and security.

In 1068 William I, returning from York, diverged from the Ermine Street to visit Cambridge and, as he had done at Lincoln and Huntingdon, ordered a castle to be erected there, on the strategic site selected earlier for the Roman camp. By 1170 it could be used as a base for the campaign against Hereward, and in the various rebellions and civil wars of the 12th and 13th centuries it was occasionally mentioned. Ralph of Norfolk encamped there in the rising of 1074–5, but preferred to make his stand at Norwich. Geoffrey de Mandeville sacked the town with great savagery in 1142, but did not apparently occupy it. In 1173 and 1174 the castle was put in repair and garrisoned with knights, at the time of the great rising of 1174 in which the Earl of Huntingdon, master of Huntingdon castle, was implicated. In August 1215 John sent directions for its safe custody, putting it under the command of Fawkes de Bréauté, and in November the bailiffs were credited with expenditure in 'enclosing' the town south of the river and providing arms for its defence. In spite of this the town was raided in the following June by the adherents of Louis of France and 20 serjeants in the castle taken prisoner. John himself came through Cambridge twice in the ding-dong fighting of his last year, and Louis held a council there in January 1217 while the young Henry's supporters were meeting at Oxford. In the fighting after Evesham Cambridge once again became the centre of military activities. The Disinherited from their camp at Ely used Cambridge as a supply base, buying up the corn which had been brought into the town from the neighbouring villages, selling their loot in Cambridge, quartering themselves on Barnwell Priory, blackmailing the town to the tune of 300 marks, holding individuals up to ransom, pillaging the Jewry, slaughtering the Jews, and carrying the chest of chirographs off to Ely. In February 1267 King Henry himself came from Bury St. Edmunds, and spent the whole of Lent at Cambridge, conducting a somewhat half-hearted campaign against the islanders and reorganizing the defences of the town. 'He caused gates to be made and ditches to be dug round the town with great diligence, not allowing the workmen to rest on holy days.' The existing town ditch was deepened and its line may have been altered, for houses were pulled down to make room for it and for an eight-foot wide walk running alongside. Nevertheless when Henry left Cambridge in April there were more raids, with destruction both of houses and of the new defences, and it was not until July that the islanders finally surrendered to the Lord Edward who had come from the north with fresh forces. The long-drawn judicial inquiries arising out of the award of Kenilworth were conducted by Walter of St. Omer in 1269–70, who made himself almost as unpopular with the Barnwell canons as the islanders by quartering himself and his family on the priory for a whole year.

It is significant that the centre of interest in 1266–7 is the market town on the level, not the castle on the hill. As early as 1232 the Barnwell chronicler thinks of it primarily as the place where the sheriff keeps his records 'If we have our own list of royal dues at the priory, we shall not need to go up to the castle to consult the sheriff's roll.' Whatever may have been the case in the 12th century, by the 13th the castle was more important as a gaol and an administrative centre than as a fortress. This development corresponds to the growing independence of the Borough, which in its turn is the measure of its growing wealth. There are many indications that it was the corn trade that came first, for instance, Picot's mills and the fines, running up to 10 marks in some instances, imposed on over 60 townsmen in 1177 for the unlicensed transport of grain.

Other indications of the importance of Cambridge in local trade are the grant of the monopoly of waterborne trade in the shire in 1131, and the right to take toll at Whittlesford Bridge to the south, where the Icknield Way crossed the Granta 'by reason of the market of Cambridge'; a right that involved responsibility for the upkeep of the bridge. Similarly the burgesses secured the right to hold an annual fair at Reach, to the north, near Swaffham, where boats coming up Reach Lode from the Cam made the hamlet a centre of inland commerce. The Jews of Cambridge were making a solid contribution to the Exchequer by 1159, and the list of contributors to royal tallages in

1211 and 1219 provides evidence of a number of rich burgesses. There was wealth available for the purchase of royal charters. Further indications of the economic resources of the town are supplied by the religious foundations. Barnwell Priory and St. Radegund's may have been given their sites by great men like Pain Peverel or Malcolm of Scotland but their endowments came from the many small gifts of individual burgesses like Hugh Domesman, Hervey fitz Eustace, William le Moyne, or Hugh fitz Absolon.

Whichever story of the origin of St. John's Hospital is correct, it was founded by a Cambridge burgess or burgesses, and maintained by similar benefactions. Town advowsons also were bestowed on religious foundations, for most of the medieval Cambridge churches seem to have been founded in the 12th century or earlier by burgesses, 'sometimes clubbing together in a guild'. The deeds of gift indicate the close connexion of town and county at this date; many of the donors bear the names of neighbouring villages, though resident in the Borough. A royal form of endowment was another source of wealth. The little leper hospital of St. Mary Magdalene, set up at Sturbridge by the townsmen in the first half of the 12th century, was granted a fair by John about 1211; it was to grow into one of the greatest in England. A fair was granted to the nuns of St. Radegund by Stephen, and Henry III confirmed John's grant of Midsummer Fair to Barnwell. And last, but by no means least, the coming of the clerks, first specifically mentioned in 1209, reinforced by the establishment of the six orders of friars between 1224 and 1290, brought custom and profit to the town, though it also produced friction, disorder and feuds.

The history of the long-drawn-out rivalry of the communities of clerks and laymen, as a succession of royal charters to Borough and University defined their rights and duties, is told elsewhere. In the early days of the Cambridge schools we hear principally of the outbreaks of individual clerks, who took full advantage of the political uncertainties of the period 1258–70, and were constantly giving trouble by their private vendettas among themselves as well as with the townsmen. The commissions, like those of 1249 and 1260, for inquiry into brawls in Cambridge, and the records on the plea rolls of the doings of the clerks, are the best evidence of the trouble caused by this unstable element, liable to be suddenly reinforced by external circumstances. Thus in 1261, although a special commission had been appointed to deal with the clerks, there are presentments before the justices in eyre of seven clerks for violence and bloodshed, committed in some instances against their fellows .

As clerks they are not in frank-pledge; as clerks if they appear before the justices they are claimed by the church. Again, the rolls of the eyre of 1272 record a story going back to 1261–4 of a group of clerks plotting to burgle the house of a Cambridge vintner at Hauxton, and being betrayed by four of their fellows to the sheriff who, with the steward of the Bishop of Ely, catches them in the act and carries the decapitated heads of the criminals to Cambridge Castle. 'Malefactors from the University of Cambridge' are declared by another sheriff in 1270 to have caused damage and expense amounting to £40 during the islanders' war. The joint arrangements for keeping the peace negotiated by the Lord Edward in 1270 were long overdue.

If the picture of Cambridge supplied by Domesday Book is tantalizingly sketchy and the historical evidence for the next two centuries fragmentary, the Hundred Rolls of 1279 present an almost embarrassingly detailed picture of the town. In March of that year Edward I ordered a comprehensive inquest into all fiefs, holdings and franchises throughout England, whether held by subjects or by the Crown. Returns survive from parts of six counties; Cambridge is the only town for which they are complete. They show that the 373 house plots of 1086 had increased to 535; they detail the trading and governmental rights of the burgesses and their grievances against the University, and they throw invaluable light on the status and history of the burgess families from whom the town officials were recruited.

One recent event to which the Hundred Rolls allude is the expulsion of the Jews. On 12 January 1275 Eleanor, the widow of Henry III, had obtained from her son the concession that no Jew should dwell in any town that she held in dower; Cambridge being one of them, the Jews of Cambridge had been deported *en masse* to Huntingdon, and it would seem that the Cambridge houses had escheated to Eleanor. Apart from this, the reigns of the three Edwards were comparatively uneventful. The justices in eyre visited the town in 1286 and 1299, as did Edward himself in 1293 and Isabel, his son's wife, in 1326, on her way from Harwich to Bristol, to dethrone her husband. The castle was rebuilt 1285–99, and the clergy of Ely diocese met in the town in 1337. The Black Death of 1349 carried off the Prior of Barnwell, three masters of St. John's Hospital, as well as almost half the scholars of King's Hall, and emptied the parish of All Saints by the Castle.

The Borough was called on to supply contingents for the Scottish and French wars nine times between 1318 and 1350, evoking protests from the burgesses. In 1338 they complained to the Council that the king's purveyor had taken their beasts for the victualling of the *Christopher* for foreign parts. As far back as 1291 there had been 'contentions and discords between the poor and the rich' in the town as to the inequitable incidence of tallage, but the chronic source of discord was the presence of the clerks, with whom serious clashes occurred in 1304, 1322, and 1371. The trouble went beyond sporadic outbursts. The lawlessness and the economic needs of the clerks had brought about the creation of an economic, judicial, and police authority rivalling that of the Borough, while, as time went on, the new collegiate foundations diverted the generosity of kings, magnates, and even burgesses from older town beneficiaries. Thus when the Peasants' Revolt reached Cambridge, its peculiar local form was determined by the fact that University and colleges as well as landlords and government officials had run up a score of ill will, so deep as to explain why Cambridge was one of the six towns exempted by name from the general pardon of November 1381.

There is evidence of considerable unrest in the town before the outbreak of June 1381. In December 1380 special instructions were sent to the Mayor and bailiffs to proclaim and enforce the peace statutes, since 'roberdesmen' and 'wastours' were causing disorder and making confederacies and unlawful conventicles in the town. On 5 February 1381 five Cambridge men were bound over in £100 to keep the peace and make no conventicles or congregations. The following day sixteen prominent burgesses were required to enter into recognizances in £100 each before Sir Roger Scales that they would be obedient to the king's justices and commissioners in the town and not obstruct the holding of their sessions by unlawful conventicles. Two of them, John Cotton, and the Mayor, Edmund Lister or Redmeadow, had been members of Parliament for the Borough in 1380. Lister had also served as county coroner and was on the Borough commission of the peace. If the two deeds surrendered by Lister in the December Parliament and enrolled on the Parliament roll are correctly dated it would seem, as Powell infers, that Lister had led a successful attack on the University six weeks before the outbreak in June. The narrative of events in the charge against him in Parliament, however, appears to assign the extortion of the deeds to Sunday, 16 June, and it is difficult to believe that the University would have kept quiet so long about its wrongs.

Though there was abundance of inflammable material within the Borough, the explosion seems to have been touched off from outside, where local agitators like Greystone and Staunford were in touch with London. But Borough and shire were interlocked. Roger of Harleston, one of the main local objects of hatred, was a burgess as well as county member. Men from the county joined in sacking his town house, and the attack on his house at Cottenham on 9 June, the first overt act of the rising in Cambridgeshire, was led by a Cambridge man, Richard Martyn. It was alleged in Parliament that the townsmen went out into the county on 16 June to fetch the enemies and traitors to the king into the town to give aid in their misdoings. John Hanchach of Shudy Camps, the ringleader in the southern part of the county, had friends in the Borough; John Giboun the younger with Richard Asshewell led a body of 160 horsemen from the town on Saturday, 15 June to join in the attacks on Shingay hospital and Thomas Hasilden's manors at Steeple and Gilden Morden.

Robert Beylham, one of those who had been bound over on 6 February, is described by the jurors in July as having induced the

Mayor to lead the attack on Barnwell, whilst Robert Brigham, an ex-Mayor, and Hugh Candelsby, one of the bailiffs, are also named as ringleaders. But the mayor's own account implies that the pressure upon him was exerted by smaller men with less well-known names, and other witnesses bore this out. The crowd of 1,000 who compelled the Mayor, as he alleged, to lead them to Barnwell probably included many from the shire.

When in December the ex-Mayor had to answer for his actions in Parliament, it was asserted that the expedition to the Mordens was by the common consent of the Mayor, bailiffs, and community. This was stoutly denied by the Mayor and bailiffs, but there was more colour for asserting communal responsibility for the next proceedings. When the raiders returned to Cambridge a meeting was summoned by proclamation to the Tolbooth at 10 p.m. James of Granchester, elected captain there, was certainly no willing ally; he was later put on the commission of 10 August to inquire into the plundering of University property.

He and his brother were made freemen of the Borough perhaps the earliest instance of honorary freedom. After counsel, it was agreed that the house of William Wigmore, esquire bedell of the University, should be destroyed and that he should be slain, if found, and that same night Corpus Christi College was raided and its muniments burnt; according to Fuller because the town resented the large number of 'candle-rents' payable to it. Besides University and college property, the houses of various burgesses were looted on Saturday. Roger Blankgren of Bridge Street took sanctuary in St. Giles Church, and his wife paid a fine to save the house a pernicious example to others, according to the jurors. The two houses of John Blankpayn, three times Mayor and four times Member of Parliament for the Borough and poll-tax collector, were sacked one in the market and one in Petty Cury.

The close of Isabel St. Ives and the house of Roger Harleston were also attacked and Harleston's dovehouse burnt to the suffocation of the doves. A Roger of Harleston, either this man or his father, had been Mayor of Cambridge and official to the Archdeacon of Ely, and had also done legal work for Warin of Bassingbourn and Hugh le Zouch. He had served as Member of Parliament for the shire in all the Parliaments from 1376 onwards, justice of the peace for both shire and Borough, commissioner for enforcing the Statute of Labourers and poll-tax commissioner. His house in Cambridge near the king's ditch was still standing in 1592–4. Besides the house at Cottenham, attacked on 9 June, he had houses at Haslingfield, Milton, Stapleford, and Denny which were ravaged on 16 June, and also lands at Coveney, where the men of Ely were seeking him. He seems a clear case of a *nouveau riche*, who had acquired standing first in the Borough, where the 14th-century terrier records him as a new-comer in the town fields, and later in the county, where his speculation in land is recorded by the close rolls. He was put on the commission which administered summary justice on the ring-leaders at Cambridge on 8 July and 24 August. He is one more instance of the type of Cambridge burgess who recurs from the days of Hervey fitz Eustace to John Mortlock, who doubles the role of squire and burgess and has all the gifts of the successful capitalist. The attacks on him in 1381 illustrate admirably the relation between the revolt and the social, economic, and administrative *sequelae* of the Black Death.

Roger Harleston was a dangerous enemy, but it was the attack on the University which brought the heaviest penalties on the town. The attack on the bedell's house was merely a beginning. On Sunday morning, while the countrymen were streaming in for their share of the plunder, mass at St. Mary's was disturbed by the Irruption of a crowd led by John Giboun, who broke open the University chest kept in the church and burnt and destroyed the muniments in it. Jewels and vessels were also seized and sold to John Giboun the elder for 10s.

The mob went on to the Carmelites' house, on the site of the later Queens' College, and broke open a second University chest containing books and other property valued at £20 by the jurors. Then, according to the relation on the Parliament roll, the Mayor and bailiffs compelled the masters and scholars of the University to make out two deeds, the first renouncing all privileges granted to the University 'since the beginning of the world to this day' by the kings of England and promising to conform to the law and custom of the Borough of Cambridge and giving security in £3,000 to pay all costs connected with the litigation then proceeding between the University and the town; the second promising to abandon completely all actions real and personal against the burgesses.

The deeds were sealed with the common seal of the University and with the seals of all the colleges. In accordance with this release the University and colleges had to surrender their charters of privilege and other deeds which, with seals broken and cut to pieces, were burned in the market place. One chronicler tells of an old woman who tossed the ashes of the parchments to the winds, chanting 'Away with the learning of the clerks, away with it.' This ritual bonfire, which accounts for the gap in the early archives of the University, corresponds to the destruction elsewhere of manorial rolls; the burgesses saw themselves as breaking the fetters of years.

On 17 June a crowd assembled on the Greencroft. Led by the Mayor, they marched on Barnwell, where they broke down the walls and palings of the prior's close, and the watergate, cut down and carried off trees, sedge, and turf and did other damage. According to the account given by the Mayor to the justices in July, he was acting under constraint and in doubt as to the attitude of the king. The community of Cambridge, he pleaded, knew that the commons of Kent, Essex,

Hertfordshire, and London had risen, with no treasonable purpose but with the consent and knowledge of the king. A crowd of 1,000 from the Borough, the county, and from other counties had assembled and declared to him, 'You are the Mayor of this town and the governor of our community; if you will not carry out our will and command in all things enjoined on behalf of the king and his faithful commons, you shall be straightway beheaded!' They brandished axes and swords and compelled him to fulfil their will, namely to assert their ancient rights of driftway and pasture in the meadows which the prior had fenced and planted with trees, and thus, coerced by threat of decollation and possibly genuinely credulous of the tale that King Richard was on the side of the insurgents, he made a proclamation to that effect. As Maitland points out, the claim to the driftway from Midsummer Green to Sturbridge Green was not new; it had been raised at the time of the great inquest of 1274–5. The prior alleged later that he had been compelled to enter into a bond for £2,000 under the common seal of the priory.

This was the last large-scale riot. The looting of houses in the Borough, as in the county, was not all over. The house of the Friars Minor was attacked, and as late as 22 June a ship coming from Reach to Midsummer Fair was plundered, but the arrival of the Bishop of Norwich with a band of armed men set a term to the revolt. On 23 June a commission was issued to Hugh le Zouch and eight others to proclaim the king's peace and the official denial of the rumour that the rebels had his authorization, to forbid unlawful assemblies and arrest insurgents.

A succession of commissions followed for inquiring into the wrongs of the Prior of Barnwell, the University, Thomas Hasilden and others whose property had suffered and for dealing with the trespasses, felonies, and treasons committed by the rebels. On 8 July the justices began their sessions at Cambridge. Few of those charged with specific offences bear names familiar in the Borough records. Richard Martyn, Robert Brigham, and John Refham who were pardoned belonged to burgess families; John Giboun who was hanged on the testimony of John Giboun the Elder was a man of some substance with friends in York, and had been involved in a lawsuit with Roger of Harleston. Giboun was in fact the only burgess executed; John Shirle, summarily tried and hanged in Cambridge on 16 July for his bold protest in a Bridge Street tavern that day against the execution of John Ball, came from Nottingham.

No officials except Hugh Candelsby, one of the bailiffs, and the Mayor himself are charged, unless R. Asshewell 'serjaunt' was one of the serjeants at mace. As the justices recognized the undesirability of depriving the community of its legal head, the Mayor was bailed and the collective responsibility of the burgesses was reserved for judgement in Parliament. But the eye of authority was on the town, and when in September John Marshall, one of those bound over in February for obstructing the justices, was elected to succeed Edmund Lister as Mayor, he was removed by royal writ, and Richard Maisterman, one of the sufferers from the revolt, was chosen to replace him.

On 2 November the Parliament opened, and on 11 December Edmund Lister with the four bailiffs of 1380–1 together with Maisterman and his four bailiffs appeared before it, together with three other burgesses representing the community, to answer for the doings of June. However much they might try to disclaim responsibility they could not get away from the fact that the two fatal deeds, sealed by the University, were in their possession. The deeds were surrendered in Parliament and formally quashed and cancelled. Nor could the late Mayor and bailiffs deny their presence during the attacks on the University and on Barnwell. After a futile attempt to dispute the jurisdiction of the court they submitted to the king's pleasure and the liberties of the town were taken into the king's hands. Maisterman was appointed *custos* for the king until Parliament should reassemble in the new year. On 17 February the king, with the assent of Parliament, gave to the University the jurisdiction hitherto exercised by the town over the purchase and sale of food and drink, and on 1 May 1382 he restored to the Mayor and bailiff all the other former liberties of the Borough, increasing its farm from 101 marks to 105. As the University paid a fee-farm rent of £10 for its new privilege, the Crown made £11 13*s*. 4*d*. a year out of the transaction.

Maisterman served as Mayor until Michaelmas 1387, though a royal writ of 28 November 1382 requiring the bailiffs and burgesses to be obedient to him suggests a restive community. In 1387 Robert Brigham, one of the pardoned rebels of 1381, was elected Mayor, as was John Marshall in 1392. In 1394 the Prior of Barnwell complained of lawless conventicles at Midsummer Fair, but apparently nothing serious occurred. The memories of the revolt were being allowed to fade out; but the relations of the University and the town had been lastingly embittered by the injuries both had suffered.

The following century was for Cambridge, as for most English towns, a period of retrogression and decay. Two bad fires, as the burgesses alleged in 1385, led to the departure of many residents. In September 1388 a Parliament was held at Cambridge; the king lodged at Barnwell Priory, various nobles stayed in the Carmelites' house, and the Convocation of Canterbury met in St. Mary's. As in 1267, a protracted royal visit led to orders for the cleansing of the town, and it may have contributed to the passing of a sanitary statute.

The outbreak of plague in the following year may have resulted from the overcrowding of the town, but as the 15th century advanced such visitations are noted more and more frequently. Henry VI, probably in September 1444, sent the Marquess of Suffolk to Cambridge instead of coming himself to lay the foundation stone of the first chapel of King's College 'for the aier and the Pestilence that hath long regned in our said Universite'.

In 1446 the burgesses, in a petition to have their subsidy assessment reduced, had represented that a number of houses were standing empty, and that many of the craftsmen in the Borough were departing because sites acquired for King's College and for students' lodgings were exempted from taxation and the rest of the town was unduly burdened. The assessment was accordingly reduced from £46 12s. 2½d. to £20, a concession confirmed in 1465. Another sign of impoverishment was the reduction, by common agreement, of the payment to the Borough Members of Parliament to one shilling instead of the statutory two, an arrangement lasting from 1427 to 1563.

Cambridge was not the scene of fighting during the Wars of the Roses; the chief sign of the times is the courting of various magnates by gifts. Among the names that recur in the town treasurers' accounts are those of Sir John Tiptoft, the Duke of York and the Duke of Norfolk. Rewards to the minstrels of various noble lords, from 1423 to 1485, do not necessarily imply the presence of their masters. The practice of looking for influential patrons, which was soon to transform the office of Recorder and create the office of High Steward, was well advanced, and the frequent references under Henry VII to John de Vere, 13th Earl of Oxford and commissioner of array for the eastern counties, anticipate pretty closely those to Sir John Hynde and Lord North in the days of Henry VIII and Elizabeth I. Under the Yorkists, royal visits became more frequent. Edward IV marched through Cambridge ten days after his accession on his way to Pontefract, and visited the town again in March 1462 and February 1464, when he granted a pardon to the ringleaders of a demonstration against the justices of the peace in the preceding January. Richard III was there in 1483 and 1484. The visits of Henry VII, 'honorably received' by town and University in 1486, as of his wife and mother, were very probably connected with their academic foundations and benefactions.

This hospitality, not to say lavishness, of the town fathers is one of many signs of reviving prosperity. The enhanced importance of Sturbridge Fair is even more significant. In 1376 the feast of the dedication of Holy Trinity Church had been put back to 9 October, because the business of the parishioners in fair time prevented due celebrations; in 1507 the date of the election of town officers was advanced to August for similar reasons. In 1516 the fair, which had originally been for two days only, was said to last from 24 August to 29 September. In 1542 Cambridge was one of several towns whose Mayor and aldermen were empowered by act of Parliament to build upon town sites occupied by decayed houses, if within 6½ years their tenants or landlords had failed to do so.

The Cambridge Paving Act of 1544 describes Cambridge as 'wele inhabyted and replenysshed withe people', but by 1584 the Privy Council was exhorting the Vice-Chancellor and Mayor to check the private enterprise of the builders and of the landlords 'who divide one house into many small tenements' and the complaints of overcrowding recur constantly from this time onwards. Thus in 1616 the University protested that the town had abused its powers of building by 'pestering every Lane and Corner with unholsome Cottages'; their statistics for 1632 give facts about the subdivision of old tenements and estimate the additional population so accommodated at 1,728 persons in the six parishes of St. Andrew, Trinity, St. Giles, St. Clement, Little St. Mary, and St. Bene't. In Green Street, St. Michael's parish, 32 families of 151 souls were living in 26 houses. The population of Cambridge, it is clear, had in the 16th century more than recovered from the setbacks of the 14th and 15th, even though the majority of the newcomers may, as Maitland thinks, have been employed in agriculture.

For all the ceremonial burning of Luther's books in 1520, Cambridge was a nursery of the Reformation. The story has been told elsewhere. Launched by Prior Barnes of the Austin Friars in a sermon addressed 'to a town audience in a parish church' at Christmas 1525, tossed back and forth by Friar Coverdale and his friends in the White Horse tavern, pushed on by later sermons of Latimer and Ridley, with Cranmer at

Jesus College to forge the dangerous link between learning and politics, broadcast by the books sold in Sygar Nicholson's shop, the new doctrines took hold of the town as well as of the University. The Dissolution of the religious houses involved a further transference of property into academic hands. Only the oldest and wealthiest of the religious houses, Barnwell Priory, lay too far out to be adaptable for academic purposes in 1538. It had made over Midsummer Fair to the town in 1505. Its buildings and property were sold to a layman, and the ancient stones were carried off to build new houses.

Of the political revolutions that accompanied the religious revolution Cambridge had a brief taste in 1553, when Northumberland, having secured the proclamation of his daughter-in-law, Jane Grey, as queen, came to Cambridge with an army to anticipate Mary's move on London. He arrived on 15 July, but Mary had eluded him and he found small support in any quarter. Late on the 20th news came that the Council had accepted Mary. In a last attempt to save his skin he went to the market-place and, standing by the market cross, himself proclaimed Mary as queen, throwing up his cap and leading the cheers hysterically. But within the hour instructions arrived from London to arrest him, and the order was executed, first by Roger Slegge, later a somewhat notorious Mayor of the town, and then by the Earl of Arundel, and the duke, his sons and adherents were next day carried off prisoners to London.

The Cambridge crowd that witnessed these proceedings had little cause to love Northumberland, for it was he who four years before had been sent to put down the second peasants' rising, known as Ket's Rebellion. Though less violent in Cambridge than in Norfolk, the character of the disturbances here is of great interest. The bitter and protracted quarrels of town and University and the quarrels of Protestants and Catholics were to the rioters of 1549 far less important than the quarrel between inclosers and commoners.

On 10 July 1549 a body of some hundred malcontents assembled by beat of drum and set to work to pull up the stakes which fenced in the new inclosures on the green commons round the town and threw them into the river to go 'jumbling and tumbling' down to Chesterton and the castle. Once again a crowd marched to Barnwell, but the prior was no longer there; it was an ex-bailiff whose hedges the rioters were tearing down, and the Mayor, far from leading them, was temporarily allied with his traditional enemy, the Vice-Chancellor.

Besides reflecting the general social and economic issues of the time, the rising throws into strong relief the divergence of interests between 'the incorporation of the town' and 'the whole inhabitants of the town'. Those charged with unlawful inclosure included leading burgesses, Mr. Recorder Hynde, ex-Mayors, and common council men, and a ballad attacked 'the false flattering freemen of Cambridge, the open and secret enemies of the poor'. The inhabitants of the crowded tenements had no share in the government of the town; as the University feared, they might well become a charge on their neighbours. The rebels had their songs not as terse as the watchwords of 1381, but giving the gist of their grievances. 'Jack of the North' states his aim:

Common to the commons again I restore Wherever it hath been yet common before. The rebels went to the tolbooth and some of them to the gallows; the Earl of Warwick had a gift from the Mayor and aldermen; the town watch received a bonus for their services. But it would seem that subsequently the principle was accepted that inhabitants as well as freemen, even though they had no ploughland, had a right to use the commons, and a town ordinance of 1583 provided for the equitable rationing of the grazing lands among the resident householders and ratepayers of the town.

Modern History

After the social unrest that engendered Ket's Rebellion, and the violent swings of the religious pendulum under Edward VI and Mary, registered, for instance, in the parish books of Great St. Mary's, Cambridge settled down to enjoy its prosperity and civic pomp, concerning itself little with national politics. When in 1564 Elizabeth I visited Cambridge, the church bells rang, and the Mayor and aldermen rode out to meet her between Newnham and Grantchester and presented her with a standing cup of silver gilt containing 40 angels. As soon, however, as the cortège reached King's College the civic representatives had to fall out, having 'no authority or jurisdiction in that place', and the rest of the celebration was the University's affair. The burgesses could well afford the purchase of the charters of 1589, 1605, and 1632, no less than the frequent gifts to the noble patrons to whose support they looked in their unceasing disputes with the University. The ill-feeling between town and gown was to take on a fresh colour in the 17th century and to be absorbed into the national conflict. With some important exceptions, the University was high church and royalist, the town puritan and parliamentary.

Though we may see a sign of the times in the ordinance of 1612 that provided that the election of the town officials should be adjourned if 16 August fell on the Sabbath, it is probable that the first note of the battle was sounded from the pulpit. The will of Alderman Faune in 1551, providing for an annual sermon to be preached before the Mayor and aldermen, had shown the changing direction of civic piety and political or religious propaganda.

A 'publique pracher' to the Borough was already an established institution before 1610, when the minister, churchwardens, and parishioners of Trinity parish invited Dr. Sibbes to accept their church for his exercises. The royal prohibition of 'new erected lectures that might draw scholars away from catechising' ended Sibbes's tenure in 1615, but after a short interval the town lectureship was revived. Financed by the subscriptions of the townsmen, who filled the newly erected galleries at Holy Trinity, it was held by a succession of eminent puritan divines. In 1624 Dr. Preston refused the bishopric of Gloucester, offered him as an inducement to abandon the post of town lecturer at Trinity. Another attempt to suppress it in 1630 broke down when it was represented to the Secretary of State that the University sermon at St. Mary's would be impossibly overcrowded if the town sermon, customarily held at the same time, were discontinued. A diatribe on Cambridge Tradesmen of the year 1640 ends:

And if this vexe 'um not, I'll grieve the Towne With this curse: States, put Trinity Lecture downe! In 1657 the town lecture was being given every Wednesday afternoon at Trinity Church, being followed by a dinner at the Mayor's house, charged to the expense of the town. In 1660 the lecture was being given once more on Sundays, and the lecturer was appointed by the Mayor and paid by the town. In 1662, however, when the Corporation was being purged, attendance at the preaching of Senior, the town lecturer, was the decisive argument for the removal of Alderman French from the bench.

Politics were permeating other churches; even in the University church the preachers laid themselves open to censure for disloyal or insubordinate observations and in 1636 a long list of disorders there and elsewhere in Cambridge was submitted to Laud. On the other hand Dr. Beale, the Vice-Chancellor, was reported to the Short Parliament in 1640 for a sermon preached in 1635 'against freedom and liberty' it was even asserted, 'against the power of parliaments'.

It was in the same year that the town, which had paid its contributions to the ship money levies of 1635 and 1636 without protest, gave evidence of nonconformity in politics as well as religion. In the election to the Long Parliament in October 1640 the burgesses not only preferred their newly admitted freeman, Oliver Cromwell of Huntingdon, their member in the Short Parliament, to the brother of their High Steward Lord Keeper Finch, but they also rejected his other nominee, Meautys, clerk of the Privy Council, in favour of John Lowry, one of the Common Council, later a colonel in the parliamentary army, and nominated as a judge in the trial of the king.

The election of a wealthy local squire in place of a government official registered the close connexion of Cambridge with a county which was petitioning against episcopacy. Cromwell's support of the commoning rights of the St. Ives freeholders broadened the basis of the new member's local popularity, and when the two Cambridge members sent down a declaration in favour of the true reformed Protestant religion, the privilege of Parliament and the liberties of the subject in May 1641, it was signed at the next Common Day by nine of the aldermen and most of the commonalty. The minority in the Corporation was again routed when at the election of officers in August 1641 Lord Keeper Coventry's orders of 1629 were repealed so that the electors should be free to choose whom they would for Mayor.

From 1638 to 1650 the Mayors of Cambridge were good parliamentarians, most of them serving on one or more of the local committees under the Eastern Counties Association, but one of them, Robert Twells, served as Mayor three times in five years. The vote of twenty nobles to the two Members of Parliament for their 'extraordinary pains' in January 1642 stands in contrast to the grudging bell-ringing and bonfires which celebrated the king's return from Scotland in the previous November, 'we being commanded thereto by the justices'.

By March 1642 the control of the militia had become not only the serious concern of the Cambridgeshire gentry but the burning issue between king and Parliament. It was at Newmarket in March 1642 that Charles gave his final refusal to the parliamentary commissioners, and he 'graciously turned in' at Cambridge to pick up his eldest son who had been greatly enjoying the hospitality of the University. But the students' loud acclamations of 'Vivat Rex!' were offset by the women and others of the town who 'followed his coach humbly and earnestly entreating that he would return to his parliament or they would be undone', as he drove from St. John's College along the Huntingdon Way to muster his forces at Nottingham.

Behind the king's back the cavaliers and Puritans were aligning themselves, and once again the strategic significance of a town which was both the centre of a strongly Puritan countryside and an important road junction became apparent. 'This place is what the enemy doth most aim at as a safe rendez-vous and an inlet into all other counties, and a means to stop the passage of provisions for London', wrote the committee of Cambridge to Speaker Lenthall in

1643. The day after Charles's departure a large body of gentlemen and commoners of Cambridgeshire and the Isle of Ely came through the town on their way to London to pledge themselves, their lives, and fortunes in defence of the Lords and Commons. Rival commands to the county militia came from king and Parliament: 'the war began on paper'. Whilst Cromwell was sending down arms to Cambridge, and moving the House that the townsmen of Cambridge should be allowed to raise two companies of volunteers and appoint captains over them, and securing a grant of £100 for the defence of the county, Charles was soliciting gifts from the University for the payment of his troops. Both sides seized arms destined for the other, bullets fired by unpractised soldiers began to make the streets of Cambridge dangerous, and in the first trial of strength between parliamentary and royalist forces Cromwell scored a bloodless, though qualified victory. The President of Clare, going by 'By-ways', succeeded in evading the 'disorderly Band of Peasants on Foot' who were guarding the Huntingdon Road at Lollworth Hedges, and carried part of the college plate to the king. But Captain Docwra who arrived in Cambridge on 10 August with a troop of horse to provide a military convoy, was disarmed and imprisoned, and thus the rest of the plate was saved from being melted down to supply Charles's needs.

On 17 August the care of the town was entrusted by Parliament to Cromwell, together with the Mayor and three aldermen. He had already seized the magazine at the castle on his own responsibility, and he proceeded to organize the defence of Cambridge. By March 1643 the new works at the castle were well in hand and in July Parliament was informed 'our town and castle are now very strongly fortified, being encompassed by breastworks and bulwarks'. All bridges over the Cam except the Great Bridge and the Small Bridges were destroyed; a gun was placed on the Great Bridge and a breastwork at Jesus Lane. Something like £2,000 was spent in bringing the fortification of the castle up to date. The soldiers found it best to stay in barracks within the ramparts, as there was plague in the town, especially at Spital End, every year from 1643 to 1647.

Ten 'brave pieces of ordnance' were mounted on the works. A garrison of 1,000 was originally intended but it does not seem in fact to have exceeded 300 at the most. In fact the castle never stood a siege, though both in February and October 1643 and in March 1644 there were alarms. It was actually soon after Naseby that the royalist forces came nearest to Cambridge when Charles, advancing south from Doncaster, drove a small body of parliamentary troops out of Huntingdon and occupied Godmanchester. On 27 August 1645 some of his horses were within two miles of Cambridge. The army there was 40 weeks' pay in arrears, and owing the town £3,000, but on 26 August a force of 1,800 foot with 8 troops of horse marched out towards Huntingdon. The king however refused battle and withdrew by way of St. Neot's and Woburn to Oxford; and Cambridge, 'so faithfull and so reall' for the Parliament, could breathe again.

A Cambridge freshman, Matthew Robinson of Hull, who had come up to Cambridge that summer to study philosophy, describes how 'the bells rang backward and the beacons were fired as if Hannibal had been at the gates'. All the students took to headlong flight, but were rounded up by the rustics of the country circumjacent, 'called in on pain of death to defend Cambridge', and brought back to the town. There Mat offered his services to the governor of the castle, 'a master of arts and a captain' and was armed with sword, firelock, and bandolier, and did night duty until the king's forces were driven away and he could resume his studies. In July 1646 Cambridge ceased to be a garrison town. It had, however, been more than a military strongpoint. It had been the headquarters of the Eastern Counties Association, formed with parliamentary approval on 20 December 1642 for the mutual aid and defence of Essex, Hertfordshire, Norfolk, Suffolk, and Cambridgeshire, joined in the following year by Huntingdonshire and Lincolnshire. It was in theory a voluntary association, supported at first by the goodwill offerings of the countryside in money and arms, and had no military commander until Manchester was appointed in July 1643, with Cromwell for his cavalry commander. It had no effective council of war until August 1643. Yet it was to become in effect the military administrative authority of East

Anglia and the reluctant parent, in January 1645, of the New Model Army. This Grand Committee and its different sub-committees sat in the Bear Inn; their orders, now mostly lost, were printed in Cambridge; the aldermen of Cambridge did yeoman service on it and on the sub-committee for the town and University of Cambridge. The governor of the castle was subordinate to it. Perhaps at no other period in its history did Cambridge exercise a more decisive influence upon national events than during the years when the regionalized forces of the Parliament were being welded into one, and Cromwell's army was being born. In a contemporary phrase, Cambridge was 'a Bulwarke to the rest'.

After 1646 political currents ran elsewhere. In 1647 the king, when the prisoner of the army, stayed at Hinchinbrooke and Childerley, but came no nearer to Cambridge than Trumpington, and the great army debates of that year were at Saffron Walden and Royston. There had been no violent demonstrations against the University on the part of the townsmen, though Parliament had imprisoned some royalist heads of houses, and the Earl of Manchester, by parliamentary authority, had ejected a number of 'ill affected' masters and fellows in 1644, and others were ejected in 1650 for refusing the Engagement.

Students had been able, if they wished, though the evidence on the subject is conflicting, to continue their studies in peace, but some who were 'disaffected of parliaments proceedings' were sent away in

March 1643. The Commonwealth period passed uneventfully; the Corporation had the new responsibility of providing preaching ministers for the churches vacated by displaced Anglicans. They recommended that six of the churches, some of them in very poor repair, should be disused, and their parishes united with others. Earlier enthusiasms were being replaced by Erastianism, and though George Fox was protected by Mayor Spalding when mobbed in the Cambridge streets in 1655, Mayor Pickering had ordered the flogging of two women Friends in Cambridge market-place in December 1653 and sent two men of the Society to prison in 1654.

As regards politics the Corporation played for safety. When their High Steward, Cromwell, died, no successor was elected, and though the town found seats in April 1660 for the two candidates whom the royalists of the county had rejected in the election to the Convention Parliament, Charles II was duly proclaimed king on 11 May by Mayor Ewin, surrounded by the aldermen in scarlet, with 'acclamations of joy from all sorts', above all from the University, whose own celebrations lasted for three days.

The turn of the royalists and Anglicans had come, and the Corporation had to pay the penalty for its Puritan politics. Those rights and privileges of the University which 'in the late years of distraction had been intrenched upon by the town' were restored. In 1662 the commissioners appointed under the Corporation Act held their sessions at the 'Black Bear' and 'Red Lion' on various days from 18 July to 30 September, and displaced the Mayor, Thomas French, seven other aldermen, including two ex-Members of Parliament, Timbs and Lowry, and thirteen common council men, nominating others to fill their places. Sir Thomas Sclater, whose moderating influences saved one Puritan ex-Mayor from being forbidden to practise in the town court, has left detailed notes of the proceedings.

The years between the purging of the Corporation in 1662 and its second purging in 1687 were marked by the last and worst outbreak of plague in 1665–6, by the struggle of the humbler sects to maintain themselves in face of the alternating enforcement and suspension of the Conventicle Act, and by the mounting concern in national politics evinced in the two elections of 1679, the earliest in which the invasion of the Borough by county political interests became obvious. The story of Charles II's escape from the Rye House Plot through the Newmarket fire which almost produced an unexpected royal visit to Cambridge, was greeted with a loyal address from the Corporation, but its further repercussions were less welcome.

When the king, having routed the Whigs, set to work to capture the corporations, Cambridge found it best to surrender its liberties on 11 November 1684. The new charter, granted on 3 January 1685, defined the constitution more precisely, with the significant addition that the Crown could remove any official of the Corporation, including the common councillors, at will. Only two aldermen and five common councillors, one being the coroner, were in fact displaced, but it was under the charter of 1685 that James II in 1688 carried out a far more drastic purge. In September 1687 the aldermen had refused to unseat their newly elected Mayor in favour of James's nominee, Alderman Blackley; on 8 April 1688 the king, by Order in Council, removed the Mayor, five aldermen, twelve common councillors, and the town clerk, and on 27 April six more aldermen and twelve more common councillors, filling their places with his own nominees.

The purge was completed by the substitution of Lord Dover as High Steward for Sir Thomas Chicheley. Alderman Newton, on the bench since 1668, was one of the ejected, and his diary gives a picture of the evening consultations of the city fathers in the house of the Mayor, fetched out of the tavern to read the king's letter. The new modelled Corporation on 8 May sealed a loyal address thanking the king for his Declaration of Indulgence and undertaking to elect such members to the next Parliament as would heartily concur with it.

They followed this up by the creation of 150 freemen, largely non-resident, whose votes could be counted on. The dissenters, now free to build their meetinghouse on Hog Hill, offered more spontaneous thanks for the Indulgence; the University, fighting for the freedom to exclude Roman Catholics, was no longer loyal. James's repentance and restoration of the lost liberties and ejected officials by the proclamation of 1688 were too late to save him. As far as Cambridge was concerned the episode left an uncertainty as to the governing charter of the town not finally determined until 1789 by the judgement in *Newling* v. *Francis*.

Once William III was on the throne, calm descended again upon the Corporation, who loyally welcomed the king on a flying visit from Newmarket in 1689, condoled with him on Mary's death in 1695, and assured him of their support against the Pretender in 1701. Under Anne the temperature rose. The rivalry of Whigs and Tories produced two hotly contested elections in 1708 and 1715 and two parliamentary inquiries. The first of these elicited such evidence of bribery on both sides as to call for a new election. The second showed the strength of party passion within the Corporation itself and the lengths to which both Mayor and aldermen were prepared to go in exploiting the institutions of their Borough; in the purchase of votes, in the invalidation of meetings by deliberate absenteeism the whole technique of 18th century corruption had arrived.

There followed a period of apparent political torpor, signalized by uncontested elections to Parliament, but it would seem that the interest in politics survived. Cole speaks of 'the collars of Brawn and other good things that were packed up and directed to Berlin when the King of Prussia was in Fashion', and later 'when Wilkes and Liberty were the *Ton* and *Vogue*, hampers of wine and all the good things that the fens and county were famous for went from Cambridge to the Demagogue'. Down to the middle of the century, as will be seen later, the Borough had been content to be manipulated by a succession of county families, following the tradition which had only been interrupted between 1640 and 1660.

But by the sixties there were signs of internal divisions of a more spontaneous character, and by the seventies reform was in the air. Two at least who supported 'the old interest' equated political reform with Protestant dissent. 'The Presbyterians are at the bottom of it', said Dr. Ewin, and Cole attributed the 'Tide of Fanaticism and Rebellion' to a 'Rabble of Dissenters of various Hues and Colours'. 'Aeconomy, Alterations in the Method of Parliament and other wild and republican Schemes', he declared, 'were first engendered at Mr. Robinson's conventicle'; the Stone Yard Baptist chapel, of which Robert Robinson was pastor from 1761 to 1790. All the evidence goes to show that the Corporation of Cambridge had not been strict in enforcing religious tests.

Between the year 1699, when five common council men had been ejected for not having taken the sacrament, and 1787, when the same objection was brought against Patrick Beales, the condition seems to have been ignored. Alderman Purchas who opened the famous meeting of 25 March 1780 'with all the Confidence of a true Fanatic' came of a family 'professedly Presbyterian or Independent', four generations of which filled the position of Mayor. The legacy of puritanism was not exhausted. Thus the first manifesto of the 'New Party', put as a test to the four candidates in the parliamentary election of 1774, upheld not only parliamentary reform and justice to the American colonists, but also 'An enlarged toleration to Protestant dissenters of every denomination'.

In 1774, as the result of intricate manœuvring, the Mayor, Alderman Newling, was an adherent of the Old Party, and this assured the return of the sitting members. Next year Tunwell was Mayor, and he did not scruple to call for the support of townsmen who were not freemen to sign the protestation against the American War that went up to London from Cambridge in November 1775, though ten of the twelve aldermen signed the loyal counter-address also presented to the king in that month. Newling was again Mayor and returning officer in the by-election of 1776 when only 34 of the 135 freemen voting were for the New Party's candidate. Both on the bench and on the floor the position of the Old Party seemed secure. But a new figure was coming on the scene.

On 2 June 1778 John Mortlock, woollen draper, was admitted to the freedom for the sum of £40. This young man of 23 had two years earlier married the wealthy daughter of Stephen Harrison, a dissenting grocer recently retired from business. In 1777 he had inherited another fortune from his father. Though his wife's father was a freeman, he was the first Mortlock to become a member of the Corporation; it is possible that from the first he was aiming at political mastery. In April 1780 he was elected to the common council and in 1782 to the bench.

John Mortlock had influential connexions. One of his aunts had married Peter Goddard, later Master of Clare, a declared enemy of the Duke of Newcastle, who for him represented the old interest. His mother's brother was a fellow of Caius, and, according to Ewin, he had also a friend in Trinity. As a landholder in the county he, like the 'anabaptist' Purchas, had a vote in the county elections, and took part in the meeting held outside the Senate House on 25 March 1780 at which, to quote the *Cambridge Chronicle*, 'The voice of the people under the canopy of heaven called aloud for redress of grievances.'

More specifically the resolution that was finally carried declared: 'That your petitioners consider every system of public administration carried on by means of parliamentary corruption . . . to be as dishonourable to the upright intentions of the Crown as it is burthensome to the property and dangerous to the liberties of the people' and prayed the House of Commons 'that effectual measures may be taken to . . . abolish all sinecure places and unmerited pensions'.

A following-up committee was appointed of which, besides the Duke of Rutland and a number of county gentlemen, three Cambridge aldermen were members; Purchas, Finch, and Forlow, who had recently 'come in on the Liberty side'; and three burgesses, Anderson, Foster, and Mortlock. Cole mentions that Alderman Burleigh also recommended it to the notice of the Corporation. It was the year of county petitioning, and the resolution is easily recognized as advocating 'economical' rather than 'parliamentary' reform. Of its supporters on the Corporation only Forlow was to remain permanently attached to the New Party.

But apart from the dramatic sounding of the popular war cry, the meeting was significant as being the means by which Mortlock was brought into contact with Rutland, the challenger of the 'old interest' in county and borough, and through Rutland with his college friend, Pitt. Rutland was glad to avail himself of Mortlock's personal and financial interest on behalf of his brother, a candidate in the coming county election, and in due course, as we shall see, Mortlock was to add the town of Cambridge to the list of Rutland pocket boroughs.

In 1780, however, Mortlock had yet to make himself master of the Borough. In April 1782 he was elected alderman, and Purchas and he founded a new club at which plans were presumably hatched for ousting the Old Party. The very general terms of the charter of 1632, coupled with the unwillingness of the courts to restrict the powers of corporations, made it possible for a skilful and audacious man of property to undermine the power of the aldermanic aristocracy and base his power on the direct support of a handpicked body of freemen. The by-law that prescribed a six-year interval before a man could be re-elected Mayor was successfully defied when the courts in 1783 upheld the election of Tunwell, and its repeal made possible the monopoly of the office by Mortlock, his dependants and his sons from 1784 to 1820.

In 1784 Mortlock was elected, without a contest, to represent Cambridge in Parliament the first native since Lowry to do so. For this he had to resign the profitable office of receiver-general of the land tax for the county, and when he secured the reversion of the post for his banking partner, Francis, the alliance between himself and Purchas, who had counted on it, was at an end. Mortlock could stand alone now; in 1785 he secured the repeal of the by-law which made a quorum of six aldermen necessary for the transaction of corporation business, thus setting aside 'the old and established custom of 200 years'. In the following year, like Lowry again, he doubled the parts of Mayor and member, and carried through the by-law which, by abolishing the initial ballot, put the election of the Mayor completely under his control. The legality of these steps had been contested by the Old Party in a series of lawsuits, but successive judgements established the right of the Corporation to remodel the constitution of the Borough at will, provided the charter was not infringed.

Finally in 1788, Newling of the Old Party was elected Mayor by the old procedure, and Francis, Mortlock's nominee, by the New. Newling appealed to the Courts, and judgement was given for Francis on the grounds that the charter of Charles I had left the method of election open, and that James II's proclamation of 1688 had revoked the charter of Charles II, which had prescribed existing custom. As a last hope, the Old Party appealed to Chancery, but the application was withdrawn in December 1789. They admitted defeat, and, with some honourable exceptions, prepared to share the spoils, though not the exercise, of power.

Meanwhile in the field of national politics the 'master of the town of Cambridge' had finally, after prolonged hesitation, taken his stand with Pitt and against Fox and Sheridan. By September 1787 the deal with the Rutland interest had been effected, and Cambridge, once open to the highest bidder, had become a safe Tory seat. In the county the Yorkes and the Mannerses had reached a working compromise, but in the Borough Lord Hardwicke had been ousted. This was patent in January 1788 when, in the contest for the recordership, an event without precedent, the Yorke candidate was defeated and Mortlock himself elected. He was merely keeping the place warm for the Duchess of Rutland's brother who succeeded him in the following April, the duke himself having died in October 1787. The duchess was fully capable of watching over her son's interests, and when Mortlock applied for the Chiltern Hundreds in May 1788, a Manners connexion was elected to Parliament in his place, his opponent only securing seven votes.

From 1788 to 1835 Cambridge was under one-party administration. Mortlock was Mayor or deputy-Mayor every year until 1810; from then until his death in 1816 his two sons held office in turn. For sixteen years 'the town of Cambridge was exempt from the mortification of having its chief magistrate bear any other name than that of Mortlock'. The younger Mortlocks, however, lacked their father's ability and energy. In 1817 the management of the Borough, according to Cooper, passed to John Purchas, the son of John Mortlock's one-time ally. He was Mayor five times between 1817 and 1831. But the system, as surveyed in retrospect by the commissioners of 1833, was what Mortlock had made it. Its worst features were manifest even before 1788, and after Mortlock's death corruption was unredeemed by efficiency.

Mortlock inherited Rutland's friendship with Pitt whom, according to family tradition, he entertained festively at the bank house when the University burgess visited Cambridge. Like Pitt, he found himself compelled to sacrifice his earlier liberal ideals to the necessities of war-time administration, though, again like Pitt, he was still supporting the abolition of the slave trade in 1792. But he loved power for its own sake. He could argue with his young friend, Gunning, that 'without *influence*, which you call *corruption*, men will not be induced to support government, though they generally approve of its measures', but a less friendly critic describes him as saying to a chessplayer, 'You, sir, play with *wooden* men, I play with *real* men. I can advance my men forwards or move them backwards as absolutely as you can yours.' Even the sober and judicious Cooper declared in 1853: 'I believe that Mr. Mortlock could have made his own footman member for the town.'

Yet it may be argued that Mortlock was a good ruler for Cambridge in the hardships and hazards of the French wars. Even in peacetime he was trying to keep down the price of food by enforcing the old market regulations against forestalling, and when in July 1795 the food riots threatened to get out of hand he took steps, in co-operation with the Vice-Chancellor, to secure the sale of food and meat at a reasonable price, patrolling the streets himself. 'Mr. Mortlock continued on horseback with the mob the greater part of the day; and under the idea that they would not be guilty of any very violent excesses, if not provoked, he determined to risk the appeasing them himself, without calling in the constables, or swearing in supernumerary ones.' We do not, however, hear of Mortlock's taking any action to restrain the violence of those riotous assemblages who, from 1792 on, attacked the meeting-houses and broke the windows of his former allies, the dissenters, who were coming to be labelled republicans, levellers, and enemies to the constitution.

The proceedings of the mob even drove some Cambridge dissenters to emigrate to America. In 1798 Mortlock chaired a meeting in the Town Hall at which a voluntary military association, to be called the Cambridge Loyal Association, was formed, 'to serve without expence to government'. A rival 'Patriotic Association' had been organized the night before at a meeting sponsored by the professor of anatomy and the son of one of Mortlock's opponents of the Old Party. In the corn riots of 1800, Mortlock did not scruple to swear in the whole of the Loyal Association as assistant constables, whilst at the same time attempting once more to deal with forestallers and regrators by law. When invasion threatened in 1803 it was his eldest son who, as Mayor, presided at the meeting in the Town Hall which resolved to form volunteer corps of cavalry and infantry. An infantry corps of 450 men was formed, and recognized by the Government, and the younger Mortlock became its commandant, with the rank of lieutenant-colonel.

During the periods of greatest distress, when subscription funds for the relief of the poor were organized, no official action was taken by the Borough. The Vice-Chancellor might take the lead; the Mayor was passive. And the gargantuan feast on Parker's Piece to celebrate the return of peace in 1814, at which 5,338 pounds of beef and 700 plum puddings of 6 pounds each were consumed, was organized independently of him.

Mortlock's death in May 1816 opened the second chapter in the history of the Rutland ascendancy in Cambridge. Under less efficient domination and against a national background of political protest, the townsmen, excluded from power but not from rate-paying, grew restive and vocal. Whittred's *Letter to the Freemen of Cambridge* prepared the way in 1818 for the first contested election since 1780. A new local newspaper of liberal views appeared *The Independent Press*. The by-election of 1819, in which only two freemen had the courage to vote against the Rutland candidate, evoked a popular demonstration and a trial for riot, and in the election of 1820 the votes were only 2 to 1 against the independent candidates. The election was followed by a town meeting, held in spite of the Mayor's refusal to convene it, which appointed a committee to take steps for the recovery of the ancient rights and privileges of the unenfranchised inhabitants. This was the first of a series of meetings in which town opinion, generally hostile to the views of the Corporation, found open expression. Resolutions were carried and petitions drafted in support of Queen Caroline, for the abolition of slavery, in sympathy with the insurgent people of Spain, in favour of parliamentary reform and of the Reform Bill. The Corporation for its part was varying its loyal addresses on royal deaths and accessions with deprecations of the factious spirit of anarchy and infidel philosophy and protests against Roman Catholic relief. Its last gesture in 1834 was to resolve to unite with Norwich and other corporations to resist by all lawful means any design to wrest from such corporations their ancient liberties.

In 1789 a Cambridge pamphleteer had asserted, 'Corporations are certainly now become obsolete however serviceable they may have been in the infancy of our constitution . . . they are now lumber that ought to be cleared away'. In 1833 *The Times*, in a leading article devoted to Cambridge, said: 'Probably no judicial investigation into a public trust ever brought to light more shameless profligacy or more inveterate dishonesty . . . a more heartless disregard of the claims of the poor, in the perversion of the funds left for their benefit . . . a more insatiable cupidity in the corporate officers to enrich themselves with the corporate property or a more entire neglect of their duties and functions as magistrates than are presented by the evidence now before us.'

That the Corporation, as Mr. Starmer told George Long and John Buckle, had a right to expend the town's income on themselves without being bound to apply any part of it to the good of the town was undoubtedly the general opinion in many boroughs besides Cambridge, but few boroughs had handled their charitable trust funds so cavalierly. As to the other assets at their disposal, the Corporation had indeed regarded the soil of the town of Cambridge as their private property. Well before the days of Mortlock it seems probable that the chance of getting a lease of town land at easy rates was one of the chief advantages of being a freeman. But the terms of the leases granted from 1791 on were the more scandalous as the demand for building land was so rapidly rising. Both the New and the Old Parties had profited at the expense of the community.

As Whittred observed in 1818, the income of the Corporation ought to have doubled from the increased value of property in the last 30 years. In fact there was an actual deficit, for the Corporation was in debt to Mortlock's Bank to the amount of £1,300. By 1833 this debt had been reduced to £150, but the financial situation was even worse. In the last fourteen years, £7,500 had been spent on legal charges, not to mention £1,300 on dinners, as against some £450 spent for the good of the town. And the unenfranchized ratepayers had to pay some, at least, of the funds for dinners and lawsuits.

The health and welfare of the inhabitants of a borough were nowhere in England considered the affair of its Corporation. Mortlock might well claim that he, following in the footsteps of his ally Tunwell, had discharged all obligations in obtaining the private Act which established the Improvement Commissions in 1788. As to legal obligations, the Corporation had been indicted for not repairing Garret Hostel Bridge and the Small Bridge in 1813. When the Great Bridge, for which they were not responsible at law, was rebuilt in 1823 they had subscribed £150 to the University's £600. To the recent drainage scheme the University had contributed £2,000 and the town nothing.

As to the maintenance of law and order, the magistrates were slack, neither they nor the town court commanded respect, and the police were so inefficient that the inhabitants looked to the University rather than to the Borough for protection. In this sphere it would seem that the situation had deteriorated since John Mortlock's days.

To the ardent young Whigs who held the investigation of 1833 the worst feature of the town government, and one that explained all its vices, was its political exclusiveness. Only supporters of the Manners interest were admitted to the Corporation. Persons claiming the freedom by birth found insuperable obstacles placed in their way unless they had the right friends. In a town of over 20,000 inhabitants, only 118 were freemen; office was the monopoly of a small inner ring, and so informal and domestic were the proceedings that they became irregular. It was not uncommon for the Grand Common Day for the election of town officers to be short of the required number to hold the election ; it appeared on investigation that Mortlock's younger son, Frederick, who had been Mayor four times, had never been sworn in as a freeman. It is ironical that the career of the man mainly responsible for this state of things had opened with the support of a resolution asserting that public administration carried on by means of corruption was unjustifiable, dishonourable, burdensome, and dangerous.

Pictorial expression to the judgement of the commissioners was given in the anonymous cartoon of a local artist entitled 'The Unjust Stewards'. It represents a table surrounded by eight aldermen exhibiting every sign of dismay at the apparition of two shrouded skeletons, waving papers inscribed 'Crane's Charity' and 'Sir Thomas White's Charity', and uttering the words, 'Give an account of your stewardship or ye shall be no longer stewards.' On the wall behind hang pictures of a grossly fat 'corporator', a lean and haggard 'non-corporator', and the representation of a gallows, with the noose prepared for the criminal. The fate of the old régime was indeed sealed, but it passed 'not with a bang, but a whimper'.

The Municipal Corporations Act did not dissolve the old Corporation of Cambridge; as Maitland says, 'In 1835 it renewed its youth.' It recognized a three-century-old shift of power by changing the style from 'The Mayor, Bailiffs and Burgesses' to 'The Mayor, Aldermen and Burgesses of the Borough of Cambridge'. The number of the aldermen was reduced to ten, and that of the councillors increased to 30, elected by the ratepayers of the five newly constituted wards. Tacitly, it would seem, the Common Day ceased to be a municipal function, only meeting for parliamentary elections, and then in a number of different polling stations.

As the Reform Bill of 1832 had destroyed the Rutland ownership of the Borough, so the first elections to the new Borough Council swept away the former corporators. The men who had taken the lead in town meetings and civic protests were elected, and any former alderman who stood was defeated. The first act of the new council, after electing its Mayor, was to eject the Duke of Rutland from the High Stewardship, and then to appoint a new town clerk. The Poor Law Commissioners meanwhile had constituted the fourteen parishes of Cambridge a poor law union, whose guardians were, with the Improvement Commissioners, the chief administrative rivals of the Borough Council.

The main features of the history of the Borough since 1835 are the increase of its population from some 21,000 to some 90,000; the extension of its area from 3,233 to 10,061 acres, with the accompanying thinning out of the congested ancient heart of the town; the settlement of its century-old disputes as to jurisdiction and taxation with the University, the gradual concentration of administrative responsibilities for the various needs of one community in one authority, and the change of its style from Borough to City in 1951.

The settlement with the University in 1856 was reached after long negotiation. The tradition of joint responsibility was translated into a modern form when it was agreed that the Senate should elect 5 of its members to sit on the Watch Committee with 9 members of the Borough Council, the Mayor acting as chairman. The practice was carried a stage further in 1889. The University then agreed to elect 6 councillors and 2 aldermen to sit on the town council and was thus in effect constituted two wards for local government purposes. Since that year a number of members of the University have served as Mayor.

The Act of 1835 had provided that the powers vested in the Improvement Commissioners could only be transferred to the Borough Council if the University consented. As members of the University had been prominent in urging such a transfer, this proved no obstacle when in 1889 it was agreed to extinguish the Improvement Commissioners and pass their duties on to the Borough Council. As early as 1855 the Borough had availed itself of the powers given by the Public Libraries Act of 1853 to open a free public library in the temporarily vacated Friends' meeting-house in Jesus Lane.

The Education Act of 1902 imposed further responsibility. Meanwhile the extension of the town boundary was desirable. Though the open fields of the Domesday Borough were not yet entirely built over, to the east and south Cambridge was encroaching on the countryside. Under the Local Government Board Act the area of the Borough was in 1912 increased by 2,224 acres and its population by 15,785 persons. Three new wards were added, bringing the number of the councillors up to 42 and the aldermen to 15. Twenty-four years later the boundaries were again extended, 4,603 more acres were added and

3,380 persons. There are now 12 wards, each represented by 3 councillors, besides the 6 University councillors, and 14 aldermen, 2 representing the University.

Successive Acts of Parliament have laid so many burdens on the shoulders of the council that in 1950 25 committees and 32 sub-committees were needed to discharge them. Since 1907 the services of women have been available, and very widely used; Cambridge has had many women councillors and up to 1945 three women Mayors. Under the Police Act Cambridge and Peterborough were the only non-county boroughs to retain their own forces. By the Civil Defence Regulations of 1949 there was imposed on the Borough, together with only four other large non-county boroughs, the duty of recruiting, training, and administering its own division of the Civil Defence Corps. It is also an 'Excepted District' under the Education Act with delegated powers from the county council as the local education authority; and the Borough was recommended for county borough status by the Local Government Boundary Commission. The headquarters of the county council and two rural district councils are located in the City.

In the Second World War Cambridge became an important centre for the defence of the east coast, an R.A.F. training centre, and the headquarters of regional organization for the counties of Norfolk, Suffolk, Essex, Cambridgeshire, Huntingdonshire, Hertfordshire, and Bedfordshire. It also served as an evacuation centre. Over 7,000 were billeted by the education officer in September 1939; but a large number both of school children and of adults returned to London, so that only 1,300 remained a year later.

In February 1941 the figure rose again to 5,500, and a third movement was started by the enemy's guided missiles in September 1944. Five of the 'Schools' of the University of London were transferred to Cambridge during the war. From 1941 the armed forces of the U.S.A. were spending their leave in Cambridge, occupying various centres from the Bull Hotel to Burleigh House on the Newmarket Road; an AngloAmerican Hospitality Committee was organized by the Mayor, and the old house that had served as Foster's Bank in the 1860's became the home of the English Speaking Union.

Amongst the special measures which the arrival of immigrants necessitated was the establishment of four British restaurants. These were at the Pitt Club, St. John's and St. Andrew's halls and the Romsey Labour Club. In the years 1941–5 some million and a half meals were served. For the civil defence of the town some 100 full-time and 2,500 part-time workers were enrolled and were placed under the control of the Borough surveyor. Fire protection was organized by the deputy town clerk. Cambridge suffered only intermittently from air raids. Apparently railways were the main target, and no ancient buildings were destroyed, the town profiting by the determination in 1844–5 of the conservatives to keep the railway station well away from the centre. Bombs fell some 22 times, and 29 persons were killed. On 2 August 1945 the freedom of the Borough was conferred on the U.S. Army Air Force which, operating from bases round about Cambridge, had done so much to defeat German attacks.

Of all the meetings held in Cambridge during this war none was more notable than the conference of the three armed services held, most secretly, in Trinity College in April 1944. Then the 'Great Court positively blushed with generals' and plans were laid for the invasion of Europe.

Apart from such vicissitudes the war left a permanent stamp on Cambridge. The decision that Cambridge should be the regional headquarters for the eastern counties in case of need was taken some years before the war, and the system came into effect in August 1939 when the regional commissioner began his work. Liaison officers appointed by the various ministries arrived with skeleton staffs in the following weeks, and the regional organization built up during the war years became permanent. In 1950 it consisted of some fifteen offices representing as many departments of the central government, located chiefly in Brooklands Avenue, 'covering acres of ground and employing thousands of people'.

In March 1951, 750 years after the grant of John's first charter, the Borough Council resolved to petition the king to grant to the Borough of Cambridge the title of city. The petition was accompanied by a statement setting forth the antiquity of the town, of its civic offices and of its chartered privileges; its importance as an administrative centre for both county and region; its economic significance as a manufacturing and marketing centre; its educational and social welfare records; its cultural and material wealth; and its increase in population and area. The culminating plea was that Cambridge, alone of the six towns that were the seats of ancient universities, had no special status, in spite of the Borough's pride in its University and the cordial relations of town and gown. University aldermen and freemen of the Borough had shared equally in promoting the petition a situation that would have been inconceivable to either party in 1617 when James I had rejected a similar request. George VI was graciously pleased to grant the petition and on 24 March 1951 Cambridge became a city, incorporated in the name of the Mayor, Aldermen, and Citizens of the City of Cambridge.

David Mills

Constitutional History

Town Records, p. 29. The Earls and the Third Penny, p. 30. Town Charters, p. 31. Arms, Seal and Regalia, p. 34. Firma Burgi, p. 35. Bailiffs, p. 36. Mayors and Aldermen, p. 38. Common Council, p. 44. Freemen, p. 46. Town Assembly or Common Hall, p. 49. Town Courts, p. 51. Justices of the Peace, p. 55. Town Clerk, p. 56. Coroners, p. 58. Recorder, p. 58. High Steward, p. 59. Town Waits, p. 60. Treasurers and Town Revenues, p. 62.

Town Records

The records in which the development of the constitution of the Borough of Cambridge can be traced are not all in the keeping of the Corporation. The *Cross Book*, the compilation of which began about 1426, is at the Guildhall and contains ordinances of dates from 1328 to 1427, transcripts of the town charters and evidences and miscellaneous memoranda of varying importance from 1460 to 1728. A volume referred to in the Treasurer's Roll for 1503–4 as the *Black Book*, now lost, may have been used by Thomas Metcalfe, Mayor

1592–3. Metcalfe's book of transcripts, preserved at Downing College, was used by Cooper to supply details omitted from the *Cross Book* for his *Annals*.

Two later collections of Borough legislation are extant; the *Book of Orders* drawn up in the mayoralty of Thomas French, an official record of the town ordinances operative at that date, and a later revision dated 20 April 1686, superseding the book of 1609. A transcript of this is in the Bowtell Collection at Downing College, having been given to Bowtell by James Day who was town clerk from 1756 to 1788. It contains supplementary orders and notes up to 1788. In the Bowtell Collection also is the Wickstede Manuscript, consisting of notes made by John Wickstede, Mayor of Cambridge 1613–14, and attorney in the town court. It contains transcripts of town ordinances, deeds and lawsuits of the period 1573–1630. Orders after 1686 are also to be found in the *Common Day Book*, a most valuable series of records of the proceedings of the Town Assembly.

When Cooper was compiling his *Annals* the first volume began in 1544 and probably extended to 1582, but when H. T. Riley saw the Corporation records in 1870, the folios before 1564 and after 1577 had disappeared. The volume covering the years 1582–1610 was probably lost by 1715; but from 1610 the series is unbroken down to 1835. Cooper has drawn upon it extensively but by no means exhaustively; it is the richest source for Corporation history in the period it covers.

The original charters from 1207 are in the City archives and have been admirably edited. Records of the town courts survive from the 13th-16th and 18th centuries, including a perfect roll for the year 1294–5. There is also a series of fines levied in the town court from 1323 to 1393. These are supplemented by numerous deeds, witnessed in the town court from the early 13th century onward, preserved at Corpus, Jesus, St. John's, Peterhouse, and Trinity Colleges. Of these the Jesus deeds have been calendared.

The financial records are the most remarkable. Only a few fragments of the Mayors' and Bailiffs' accounts survive at the Guildhall and in the Bowtell Collection, but a long series of Treasurers' Rolls has narrowly escaped destruction. An isolated account for 1347, and a number of rolls for the period 1422–1514, together with an unbroken series from 1787 to 1835, are in the City archives; a series, running with interruptions from 1515 to 1787, is at Downing College in the Bowtell Collection, bound up under the title *Libri Rationales*. Cooper has drawn upon them in his *Annals*, but very selectively. Hagable rent rolls for 1483, 1491, 1493, and 1524 are at the Guildhall, and have been printed in part, and there are subsidy rolls for 1513–17. The series of Lease Books, from 1558 on, gives details of town property, and there are Inclosure awards for 1804 and 1811. There are minutes of the paving, cleansing, and lighting commissioners, set up by the Act of 1788, for the years 1788–1837.

The Earls and the Third Penny

While there is no evidence that Cambridge was ever a mediatized borough, the earldom of Cambridge seems to have been regarded as an appendage to that of Huntingdon from 1050 to 1237, and with the earldom went certain rights, and probably certain lands in the Borough. These rights, presumably exercised by Waltheof's widow Judith in 1086, were transmitted by her daughter Maud successively to her first husband, Simon de St. Liz I, her second husband, David I of Scotland ; her sons, Henry of Scotland and Simon de St. Liz II ; her grandsons, Malcolm IV, William the Lion, Simon de St. Liz III, and David of Scotland ; and her great grandson, John the Scot, with whose death in 1237 the earldom became extinct, and the lands of the Honour of Huntingdon were divided among the three co-heiresses.

The connexion of the line with Cambridge is indicated when David I is pardoned 13s. of the aid of the Borough in 1129, and more specifically when the second David is found in possession of the earl's third penny. The original charter is extant by which he granted £5 of it to Richard fitz William ; the other moiety was granted to another dependant, Simon de St. Liz, probably descended from an illegitimate son of a St. Liz earl. These moieties, regranted to various recipients, were in 1279 payable to Cauldwell Priory, Kenilworth Priory and Barnwell Priory. The town had bought out all these grantees by the Reformation, Kenilworth in 1527, Cauldwell in 1530, Barnwell at some unknown date.

That, in spite of the silence of Domesday, the early earls held land in the Borough seems certain not only from their being chargeable to the town aid but from the gift to Barnwell Priory of 2 acres of land between St. Giles Church and the river by the Countess Maud in 1092, and the gift to the nuns of St. Radegund of 10 acres of land near Greencroft by King Malcolm IV. In 1209 it is specifically stated that Earl David has 40 librates of land in Cambridge, and the half fee in Cambridge held by Leonius Dunning of Isabel de Brus in 1242, as of the Honour of Huntingdon, almost certainly represents a portion of the original holding of the earls.

When, in 1340, Edward III created William of Juliers Earl of Cambridge, granting him the castle and the revenues of the town of Cambridge and £20 a year out of the issues of the county, it had become distinct from the earldom of Huntingdon, and when revived again in 1362 in favour of Edmund of Langley it was once more subordinated to another title, that of York. Ill luck seemed to haunt the title; after the execution of Edmund's son for treason and the death of his grandson at Wakefield, it merged in the Crown, to be revived four times between 1661 and 1677 in favour of four infant sons of James Duke of York, all of whom died under the age of four.

Town Charters

It was not from earls but from kings that the Borough secured its chartered liberties. The first charter, granted by Henry I between 1120 and 1131, giving the town the monopoly of waterborne traffic and hithe tolls, also recognized the Borough court. The next step was to secure the right to collect the revenue due to the Crown. By 1185 the burgesses were ready to offer 300 marks of silver and one of gold to have their town at farm 'so that the sheriff might not meddle therewith', and Henry's writ of 1185–6 granted the town to the burgesses at the customary rate, answering for it themselves at the Exchequer. However, when Henry II died in 1189 they had paid no farm at all and were still owing £70 of the fine.

The grant, which had been made by writ, not charter, was not perpetual, and Richard resumed it, winding up the account at some sacrifice to himself. By 1199 the burgesses were prepared to try again in spite of the heavy tallages recently levied; they offered 250 marks to have their farm with such liberties as other towns had. What these were appears in John's charter of 1201, which recognized their established customs and tenures, confirmed the competence of their court, exempted the burgesses from the duellum, allowing them to use traditional methods of defence in pleas of the Crown. Their guild merchant was confirmed, with the right to *withernam*.

Their Rogationtide fair was secured to them; and they were declared free of the sheriff's exactions such as scot ale. The farm is not mentioned, but the Pipe Rolls show that they were paying it. In 1207 they offered a further payment to have their farm in perpetuity, and John's second charter granted the town to the burgesses in fee farm, adding £20 by tale to the 'old farm' of £40 blanch, and specifically giving them the right to appoint their own reeve who would be accepted as their agent at the Exchequer. In 1227 two charters from Henry III confirmed John's grants, and in 1256, besides a short charter granting a limited exemption from *withernam*, the burgesses obtained the all-important grant of return of writs, jurisdiction over pleas of replevin, and the right to elect their own coroners.

This gave them an independence of the sheriff in administration equivalent to that which they had secured in finance in 1207. Well before this date Cambridge itself had added to the officially recognized reeves or bailiffs a Mayor, who embodied the communal consciousness that was both cause and effect of its public responsibilities and privileges. Though addressed in a royal writ of 1231, it was not until 1382 that the Mayor was named in a town charter.

The charter of 1268, though granted for the advantage of the University, has to be noted for its lasting effect on Borough institutions. It was modelled on the charter to Oxford in 1255, and provided that there should be two aldermen with four associated burgesses to assist the Mayor and bailiffs in keeping the peace, who were to be sworn to the office, and two men in each parish sworn to search periodically for suspicious strangers. It also forbade regrating, and provided for the holding of the assize of bread and ale twice a year, the Chancellor of the University or his deputy being present. The two aldermen and their assessors, later called councillors, were elected annually from this time onwards along with the Mayor and bailiffs.

The charters of 1280, of 1313, and of 1377 did little but confirm previous grants. The charter of 1382 'records not an increase but a diminution of the liberties that the community had enjoyed'. In 1381 the liberties of the Borough had been forfeited for its participation in the Peasants' Revolt, and when, after submission, a new grant was made to the Mayor, bailiffs, and burgesses, the fee farm was raised from 101 to 105 marks, and the supervision of baking and brewing, of weights and measures, of forestalling and regrating and of the sale of food was taken from the town and given to the University.

Loss of jurisdiction meant loss of revenue, and in 1385 the Borough received a compassionate grant of the profits of justice arising from the fines and forfeitures imposed in the king's courts by his justices upon dwellers in the town, with the right to collect them by its own agents. A subsequent grant in 1394 provided a simple procedure for proving that no University privileges were infringed in levying these profits. The charters of 1405, 1419, 1424, and 1437 merely confirmed previous grants, but in 1446 Henry VI, as we have seen, granted a reduction of the town's assessment to the 10th and 15th which was confirmed by Edward IV in 1465.

The culmination of the Borough's evolution came about, almost accidentally, in 1530. In 1529 the Mayor and bailiffs of Cambridge appeared in the court of King's Bench to assert their claim to the goods of a man who had committed a felony in Trumpington Street in 1527 and fled. Their claim was based on the grant of 1385, backed up by the plea that 'The town of Cambridge is an ancient borough, and one of the most ancient boroughs of this realm of England and from time immemorial the said borough and town have been one body and one commonalty incorporate in itself, as well of the burgesses of the said borough and town as of one Mayor and four bailiffs by the said burgesses elected each year on the feast of St. Michael the Archangel.'

They added that from time out of mind the Mayor, bailiff, and burgesses had sued and been sued in the courts, and had been capable of purchasing and holding lands and liberties. The Crown demurred, but the court found for the town, thus recognizing

Cambridge as a corporate Borough by prescription, and the exemplification of the judgement is preserved with the royal charters in the City archives. The exemplification of 1548, recording the recognition by the King's Bench, sitting at Cambridge in 1383, of the criminal and civil jurisdiction of the town courts, is discussed below; it adds no new liberties. Elizabeth I's one charter, of 1589, securing the town's rights over Sturbridge Fair, was intended to end disputes between town and University, but could hardly do so while the University retained its jurisdiction over victuals, weights, and measures.

In 1605 the Borough obtained a charter from James I formally creating a corporation, which should be capable of holding property, of suing and being sued, of using a common seal, of making by-laws and of acquiring lands in mortmain to the value of £60 a year. The most interesting provision is that the by-laws must have the consent of the burgesses or the greater part of them, the Mayor in office being one. But neither aldermen nor common council were mentioned; it is the barest sketch of a constitution.

In 1616 when the burgesses petitioned for a charter granting Cambridge the title of city, they desired 'that in the Charter all the offices and officers of the Citty may be expressed', but nothing came of it. In 1626 a *Quo Warranto* brought against the Mayor, bailiffs, and burgesses to know by what title they claimed their liberties led them to apply for a renewal of the town charter, and in 1632 they obtained what came to be known as 'the governing charter', for under it Cambridge was to be administered until the days of municipal reform. Elastic as it was to prove under the strains and stresses of the late 18th century, the charter goes into fuller details than any previous grant. To the statements about incorporation, repeated once more, it adds the provision that there are to be 12 aldermen and 24 common councillors, without defining methods of election or selection, nor are the methods of acquiring freemanship defined, though a seven years' apprenticeship is prescribed for the practice of any craft in the Borough.

Legislation is to be in an assembly publicly summoned by the Mayor for that purpose; and he is empowered to appoint a deputy-mayor. The two town treasurers, now first mentioned in a charter, though known to exist in Cambridge as far back as 1347, may sue in the town court for money penalties incurred by those who infringe the by-laws. Finally the Corporation is given the right to levy rates for 'works necessary for the public and common good' not only upon burgesses but upon inhabitants not being members of the University and to compel payment by process in the courts.

Arms, Seal and Regalia

As early as 1270 the common seal of the burgesses is said to have been affixed to a chirograph, but in 1352 it was the seal of the mayoralty which the Mayor affixed to a deed at the request of the aldermen and brethren of St. Mary's guild. The deed is still preserved at Corpus Christi College. This seal is 1½ inches in diameter. It shows an embattled bridge of four round arches over a river. In the middle of the bridge is a gateway tower surrounded by an object which might be a crocketed spire. On either side of the tower is a shield bearing the lions of England and supported by a lion. The legend is s'illum majoritatis ville c. In 1381, when the representatives of the Borough appeared in Parliament to answer for its misconduct in the Rising, they declared the town had still no common seal, but eight years later the town was ordered to give full power to the Mayor and bailiffs under its common seal to answer for them to the charges of the University. In 1423 the Four and Twenty ordained that there should be a common seal with which all leases by the commonalty should be sealed. An impression of this seal is extant for the year 1434, whilst two fragments of it are preserved in the City archives. This seal, $1^5/8$ inches in diameter, showed an embattled bridge of four complete and two incomplete arches, with thereon an escutcheon of the arms of England and France quarterly, supported by two angels kneeling. The legend was s. communitatis ville cantebrigie. This seal was probably used until 1575 when a grant of arms to the Borough made it obsolete.

The arms now used by the City were granted in 1575 by Robert Cooke, then Clarenceux King of Arms, reproducing certain features of the 15th-century seal. They are thus described:

Arms, gules a gold arched bridge with three towers, above it a fleur-de-lis or between two roses argent, and in base barry wavy silver and azure, and thereon three ships sable, each with one mast and the sail furled.

Crest, on a wreath or and gules, a grassy mound, and thereon a silver bridge.

Supporters, two sea-horses, their bodies gules and their tails proper with gold fins.

The ships are supposed to refer to the riverborne traffic of Cambridge, and the crest, more like a castle than a bridge, suggests Cambridge castle on the hill above the bridge.

The new seal incorporated these arms, the supporting angels being replaced by seahorses, and the legend was sigillum communitatis villae cantabrigiae. A new seal in silver was presented to the town by the High Steward in 1736, and the old one was broken, but the design of 1575 is still preserved. Meanwhile a second seal of the mayoralty dating from 1471 is known. This shows a level bridge of four arches over a river and thereon an escutcheon of France ancient and England quarterly supported by two lions. The legend was sigillum majoritatis ville . . . t. The present arms without helm, crest, or supporters, were used on an oval seal of the 17th century, $1^{5}/8 \times 17/16$ inches, with the legend seal of the mayoralty of the borough of cambridge.

Most of the plate belonging to the Borough of Cambridge was sold or lost after 1835, and in 1956 the regalia apart from the maces and mayoral chains comprised a silver tankard with lid, coffee pot, stoup, and four salt cellars. The Great Mace in silver gilt dates from the reign of Queen Anne. It is 53½ inches long, and weighs 155 ounces. It was presented by Samuel Shepheard of Exning, M.P. for the Borough. Four smaller maces, made in 1723–4, were presented by Thomas Bacon, M.P. They are each 42 inches long, and weigh between 85 and 90 ounces. Finally there is a serjeant's mace of copper gilt, dating from the reign of Charles I. The Great Mace has a rest weighing 25 ounces, and the serjeant's mace a carved oak rest presented in 1903. The Mayor's chain dates from 1890, and that of the Mayoress from 1911.

Firma Burgi

The farm of the Borough was probably £30 at the time of Domesday. In 1185, when Henry II granted the town to the burgesses, the ancient farm was £40, blanch to which he added £20 by tale. This was the rate at which John granted it in perpetuity in 1207. The Exchequer records show the burgesses regularly accounting for £62 but in 1279 they say that they are also paying a new increment of £5 and several farms for houses. In the petition presented in Parliament in 1330, complaining that the market tolls on which they principally rely for the payment of the farm have been reduced in value by grants of exemption to the country lords and their tenants, the burgesses did not mention the increment. When, however, the farm was assigned in dower to Queen Isabel next year it was stated to amount to £67 9s. 10d. made up of ancient farm, increment and five small farms. When actually granted to her in March 1332 it was stated to be £67 19s. 10d. and that was the sum for which the bailiffs accounted until the Peasants' Revolt. After that it was raised to £70.

The burgesses' complaint in 1383 that the loss of the profitable assizes of bread and measures made the farm unendurably heavy led not to its reduction but to the grant of royal profits of justice. Renewed complaints in the 15th century finally elicited a reduction of the farm by £10 in 1483, but Richard III's concession was revoked by Henry VII in 1485.

There were occasional temporary grants from the farm of the Borough, but from 1235, when Henry III assigned it to his bride in case his mother should outlive him, it was customarily part of the queen's dower. It was so held by Eleanor of Provence after her husband's death, by Margaret, Edward I's second wife, by Isabel, wife of Edward II, from 1331, and by Elizabeth, wife of Edward IV, from 1466. In 1562 it was appropriated by Elizabeth I to the expenses of the household. In

1655 the Corporation bought up the fee farm for £665, £300 of which was borrowed from one alderman.

In 1660, however, they conveyed it once more to the Crown, and it was assigned to Catherine of Braganza as part of her jointure. In 1671 the reversion of it was purchased by Sir George Downing and it is now paid to Downing College.

Bailiffs

The charter of 1207 empowered the burgesses to choose their own reeve, but the first official communications were directed to more than one official. From 1212 to 1224 writs were addressed to 'our reeves' or, from 1215, 'our bailiffs' of Cambridge. The bailiffs are thus older than the Mayor, first named in 1231, and as far back as a number is traceable, they number four, a peculiarity Cambridge shares with Norwich where, however, no Mayor appeared until 1404. From an early date the names of the bailiffs may be learnt from the deeds published in the town court which they witness along with the Mayor, and both the Exchequer records and the lists compiled by Mason and Cole show that in the 13th and 14th centuries bailiffs, like Mayors, very commonly served the office several times, and that a fair proportion of them became Mayors later. Between 1270 and 1377, 19 of the 37 Mayors had been bailiffs first, but as the 14th century advanced, the office of bailiff came to be held by less wealthy and important men than those who reached the mayoralty. The bailiffs were elected annually on the same day as the Mayor.

At Norwich the four bailiffs were from the first responsible each for one of the four leets of the town. In Cambridge evidence of a similar system only appears towards the end of the 14th century. The ordinances of 1419 that none should be bailiff outside the ward in which he resided indicates that by then the office was territorialized, as is suggested by the annotations on the roll of the town court of 1389–90. The four sets of initials entered against the different pleas suggest that the execution of judgement is distributed locally among the four bailiffs. The accounts of 1510 show unequivocally that each has as his bailiwick one of the four wards, Bridge Ward, Market Ward, High Ward, and Mill Ward, for which he accounts. The orders for the election of the bailiffs in 1566 prescribe a routine for service; men are to proceed from the treasurership to the bailiwick of the Mills, the High Ward, the Market and the Bridge in that order. In 1622 it was decided to reduce the number of the bailiffs to three, the duties and perquisites of the bailiffs of the Mills being distributed among the other three. The charter of 1632 does not specify the number of bailiffs, but by 1662 there were again four.

The primary responsibility of the bailiffs was for the payment of the fee farm at the Exchequer and of the third penny to its beneficiaries, a responsibility shared by town ordinance with the Mayor from 1459 at least. The revenues available for this were the profits of the town courts, the mill and market tolls, and the hagable rents. Accounts of the Mayor and bailiffs for 1510–11 and 1523–4 show that the four bailiffs collected the dues from their four wards, and that the accounts were balanced at financial sessions called *ports*, at intervals ranging from six to twelve weeks. The order book of 1609–11 lays down that 'in consideracion of much slackness . . . used of late by the Maior and Bailiffs of this town in making and keeping their last port after their yere expired, from henceforth the Bayliffs for the tyme being shall yerely justly and truly make their last port and accompt of all somes of money and other thyngs remayning in their hands towards the payment of the fee farme of the towne before the Maior last before . . . at any time within one whole week between Michaelmas and Christmas at the appointment of the said Maior, he to give warning four days before'.

Besides their external obligations, the bailiffs' financial liabilities included payments to the Mayor and to the Recorder, presents and fees to the justices of the peace, and the entertainment of both townsmen and visitors at dinners at election time in August, at the swearing in at Michaelmas, and in fair times. The provision of 1600 that they might not let their bailiwicks or the profits of them to farm indicates that a profit could be made on the office, in spite of the fact that their expenses for hospitality were estimated at £60 in 1622. This is borne out by an incident of the year 1605.

Thomas Thompson, one of the four bailiffs, was removed from his office at a Common Day on 17 October; according to the official return of the Mayor, because he had assaulted another bailiff who was keeper of the Tolbooth, ousted him from his custody for a week, and refused, after four summons, to appear in court or Common Day to answer to the charges brought against him. According to Thompson's own account, the Mayor had a private quarrel with him and maliciously sought to prevent him from prosecuting a plea of debt in King's Bench. The writ of *mandamus* for Thompson's reinstatement, tested 30 January 1606, refers explicitly to the 'large fees, wages, rewards, rents, tolls and other emoluments pertaining to the office'.

The bailiffs presided with the Mayor at the town courts and, as we saw, witnessed transactions in them from 1256 onwards; they had to serve the writs passed on to them by the sheriff, they levied the money penalties imposed in the courts, and they shared the responsibility for keeping the peace. In 1566 the status of the treasurer had been below that of the bailiffs, but as the importance of the town courts and of the revenues for which they were responsible dwindled the importance of the bailiffs also lessened, and as we have seen, the office ceased to be a coveted one. Instead of serving, men fined 'to pass the offices' of treasurer and bailiff, in order to become eligible for the common council and the bench. By 1833 the bailiffs' functions had become very limited. They attended all corporate meetings, and two had to be present at the sittings of the town court, but they took no part in the proceedings. The treasurer had taken over their financial responsibilities since 1795.

Their connexion with the wards had ceased, as well as their duty of enforcing the peace. They were still elected annually, only resident burgesses being eligible, and they usually served for four years. 'Persons to whom the salary is an object, and who solicit the office, are elected.' Today four of the town councillors are elected bailiffs and take precedence after councillors who are exMayors and before councillors who are ex-bailiffs. Their duties are honorary, but the fact that in a procession they precede the Mayor can be regarded as a symbolic survival of their historic priority.

Mayors and Aldermen

Some would identify the *prepositus* whom the burgesses were in 1207 empowered to elect, and also the *prepositus* who witnesses various early town deeds, as the emergent Mayor. The first dated use of the term Mayor is in the writ of 1231 addressed to the Mayor and bailiffs of Cambridge concerning scholars' lodgings; the first attribution of the name to a particular man is to Hervey fitz Eustace, who flourished about 1200 to 1240, and owned the manor-house now known as the

School of Pythagoras. He witnessed an undated deed at St. John's College as *Dominus Herveus Maior*; and in another St. John's deed and in several at Jesus College he witnessed as Hervey the alderman .

The fact that in some deeds he took precedence of another witness described as *prepositus* is attributed to his undoubted wealth or knightly standing by Sir John Milner Gray, but it is possible that here as elsewhere the Mayor, embodying a new civic consciousness, is from the first distinct from the ancient royal official who links the Borough with the royal treasury. The title alderman does not recur in this connexion, probably because the guild merchant fades out; after 1288 the alderman is a town official who assists the Mayor. But as the term *prepositus* drops out of use the term *maior ballivus* or *capitalis ballivus* is applied by the central government to persons whom the burgesses of Cambridge knew as their Mayor, and the list of bailiffs answering for Cambridge at the Exchequer from 1250 onwards certainly includes some active Mayors as late as the reign of Edward II, though it is by no means identical with the list of Mayors as far as that has been ascertained. The 'bailiff of the liberty of Cambridge' to whom in 1340 the sheriff passed on the justices' orders to arrest was the Mayor.

In spite of the labours of many scholars and the wealth of material in the deeds witnessed before the Mayors and bailiffs and now preserved in college archives, no precise list of early Mayors can as yet be drawn up. Maitland's tentative list has been revised and amplified by Milner Gray, and some further corrections should be made. Hervey fitz Eustace was dead by 1240; both Richard Crocheman and Robert Seman held the office of *prepositus* in his lifetime. Roger de Wykes between 1256 and 1260 and perhaps in 1271, and Robert of St. Edmund were certainly Mayors, but that the position was still only of local significance is indicated by the fact that the eyre roll of 1261 names four 'chief bailiffs' but no Mayor. The eyre roll of 1272 gives the names of five men who were Mayors between 1261 and 1272: Roger de Wykes; Richard Lawrence or Lorens, who was Mayor in 1263 and 1269–70 and probably at intervening dates; John le Rus, of the important family that lived just outside Trumpington Gate, Mayor not later than 1269; John Martyn, Mayor in 1270–1, and frequently between 1272 and 1278; and William Tuillet, whose name comes first on the eyre roll of 1286, which lists the five Mayors who had held office since the eyre of 1272.

William Tuillet has not been noted hitherto. He was dead by 1279, when the survey reports his purchases of land in the Cambridge fields from seven different holders, and the house in All Saints parish inherited by his son Henry, town bailiff and hundred juror. His other son, Robert, held land in Barnwell of the canons and was bailiff in 1283 and Mayor 1293. His daughter Avice married John Martyn the Mayor. Bartholomew Goggyng, Mayor 1272–4, had five houses and 22 acres of land, and was the grandson of the notable Hervey the clerk who became a canon of Barnwell. His sister Mariota married Nicholas Childman, 'chief Bailiff' in 1260. William Elyot, Mayor in 1274 and probably 1275, is inconspicuous. Three at least of John Martin's possible fifteen mayoralties fall in this period; and John Butt was holding the office for at least the sixth time when the justices arrived in 1286, and was to serve four times more before his death in *c.* 1298.

From the 1279 survey, supplemented by feet of fines and other records, it is possible, as Maitland and Gray have shown, to get a very clear picture of the typical Cambridge Mayor of the late 13th century. He belonged to one of a group of families closely linked by intermarriage, taking full advantage of the burgage tenure that permitted easy sale and purchase of land; building up estates that might soon disintegrate by improvidence or borrowing. He was very generally a member of St. Mary's guild. Not infrequently he had land in the county as well as the Borough. The same surnames recur as office holders for a generation or two; then fresh names appear. There was always room for the newcomer who could pay his way into the governing ring.

The 13th-century pattern persisted through the succeeding centuries. Of the 58 men who were Mayors between 1300 and 1500, 37 had served as bailiffs once or more often, and an equal number had represented the town in Parliament. The two last ex-bailiffs to become

Mayor were William Bright in 1571 and John Jenkinson in 1601. As the practice of dispensing burgesses from serving the lower offices for a fine became established and freedoms were bestowed on non-residents it became possible for the country gentry to exercise more influence in the Borough, but this seldom affected the choice of Mayor. Roger of Harleston, Mayor 1356–8, whose extensive holdings in the town fields were supplemented by estates at Milton, Haslingfield, Cottenham, and Denny and who represented the county in Parliament three times, a newcomer to the Borough and possibly a land speculator, is not a typical Mayor of Cambridge. As a rule, besides holding lands in the common fields the Mayor practised a trade; fishmongers, drapers, grocers, goldsmiths, innholders, wax chandlers, smiths, butchers, bakers, brewers, tanners, skinners, all held the office. Some are described as clerks, and may well have been members of the University, like Robert Brigham, Mayor 1348–50, and John Bilney, Mayor five times between 1406 and 1427. John Edmunds, Mayor 1586–7, was the son of a Master of Peterhouse. Some studied law and became town attorneys like Wickstede, Mayor 1613–14, and his son-in-law Spalding, Mayor in 1630, 1655, and 1662. Many, besides promoting 'the wealth, relief, profit, and countenance of the town' in their lifetime, made gifts to the town in their wills.

These substantial burgesses, it would seem, held office for several years in succession or turn and turn about. Between 1286 and 1299 there were six Mayors, including John Butt and John Martyn. The same pattern of office-holding continues to the end of the 15th century and the surnames recur; John Dunning, seven times Mayor between 1296 and 1309; Richard Tuylet, six times Mayor between 1337 and 1346, a succession of Morices, whose ancestors can be found in the 1279 survey, held office between 1314 and 1374, and successive generations of Brighams and Hessewells were Mayors in the 15th century.

Richard Maisterman, imposed on Cambridge by the central government after the upheaval of 1381, held office continuously to 1387; after that it was usual for the Mayor to serve for two successive years but not longer. That the office entailed heavy expenses appears from the deed executed on the election of John Hessewell in 1490, discharging him from all future service as Mayor on his undertaking to serve if re-elected until Michaelmas 1492. After 1500 it was the normal practice to elect a new Mayor each year; and in 1568 it was ordained that none should be elected who had held the office within six years preceding; an ordinance that, though not strictly observed, was not rescinded until 1782.

The earliest record of a Mayor's election is endorsed on the roll of the town court for 1295; it took place on 9 September, the morrow of the Nativity of the Virgin, and in 1383 the burgesses declared that they had elected their reeve and bailiffs on that day since 1207. In 1507 it was advanced to 16 August, the morrow of the Assumption, because of Sturbridge Fair, 'the busy time of all the burgesses', and so it continued until 1835. An ordinance of 1428 refers to the swearing in of the Mayor and bailiffs on St. Michael's Day, and as far back as 1261 the Mayor is said to serve until Michaelmas, and no other term of office is ever hinted at.

The earliest form of the oath, taken by Mayor and bailiffs alike, appears to be about 1327: to defend the liberties of the town with the help of the community, to maintain the ancient customs and ordinances of the town, to give true judgements and execute them swiftly, to keep the peace of the town and preserve the commons intact; and not to be a regrater of victuals while in office. Apart from the last clause, the same oath is in the order book of 1609, supplemented by an oath against assenting to a union with the University, and other additions reflecting current issues were made from time to time.

The method of election as prescribed in 1344 was that the Mayor and his 'assessors sitting on the bench' should select one burgess and the commonalty another; these two should elect twelve burgesses from those present, themselves excepted; the twelve should co-opt six more and these eighteen should elect the Mayor and the other officers. In 1419 the commonalty ordained that only those who had served as bailiff or treasurer might be chosen to elect the officers. The next important modification was made in 1568, by which time the status of the aldermen in the municipal constitution had been established.

In Cambridge the word alderman has at least three distinct meanings. Hervey fitz Eustace, alderman and Mayor, was probably alderman of the guild merchant recognized by John's charter of 1201 and when it was revived under Edward VI and Mary, the Mayor for the time being was again alderman of the guild. Other burgesses were aldermen of the guild of St. Mary. Secondly, under the University's charter of 1268 two aldermen of the town were to be elected annually to assist the Mayor and bailiffs in the keeping of the peace, with the help of four other burgesses. Finally in 1566 a town ordinance provided that there should be twelve aldermen at the least from whom the Mayor should be annually elected.

The evolution of the aldermen's bench was a long and obscure process. Tait was doubtful whether the six men elected under the charter of 1268 served as a Mayor's council and thought they had no part in choosing the Twenty-four in 1426. But as early as 1344 the Mayor's assessors were sitting with him on the bench; the 1426 narrative specifically mentions the Mayor's assessors and counsel; and it seems quite probable that it became customary to re-elect the same men to the office.

That the aldermen had other duties besides maintaining the peace appears from their sharing the responsibility of presiding in the town courts and of having custody of the town seal, whilst in 1462 a town ordinance is 'made' by the Mayor, aldermen, bailiffs and burgesses. The fee payable after 1499 by everyone 'chosen to be alderman or called to the Common Bench of the town' can hardly have been imposed on the annually elected keepers of the peace. There were at least four aldermen as well as the Mayor in 1509. It is between 1535 and 1545 that the aldermen come into the foreground of the town records.

Thomas Cromwell writes to them along with the Mayor, bailiffs and burgesses; town documents refer to 'Mr. Maire and his brotherne' and 'Maister Mayor and other Aldermen of the Towne'. One of the first entries in the Common Day Book records a resolution of the aldermen and the Twenty-Four; and in 1545 'all the Aldermen' attend a banquet. In 1551 'three of the auncientest aldermen' are to supervise the diking of the commons. In 1552 one of the common councillors, 'elected to the bench', refused to accept office. In 1556 an ordinance in August was approved by eight, and another in October by nine aldermen. In 1560 a distinction was drawn between aldermen who are ex-Mayors and those of lower standing. The future town council had clearly taken shape before the overhaul of 1564–8.

On 1 November 1564 a committee of the Mayor, three aldermen and three common councillors was appointed to revise the method of electing the town officers, and it would seem that the advice of the Recorder was also sought. On Hock Tuesday 1566 ordinances were approved for a trial period of two years which provided, *inter alia*, that there should henceforth be at least twelve aldermen; that one of them should be elected Mayor annually by the commonalty from two candidates nominated by the aldermen. Though the other provisions remained in force, those for the election of the Mayor were not satisfactory. Advice was sought first from the High Steward, Thomas, fourth Duke of Norfolk, and then from five Cambridgeshire gentlemen, created freemen of the Borough *ad hoc*, and with their help the ordinance of 1568 was drafted. By this two common councillors chosen by lot were to nominate the first twelve electors, who were to co-opt six more, and these eighteen persons were to elect the Mayor and officers. A time limit was fixed for each stage of the election, and in case of ties the Mayor was to have the casting vote. The electors were to swear that they had not been 'laboured' to cast their votes for or against any men. This arrangement, which increased the part taken by the Twenty-Four at the expense of both aldermen and commonalty, and sought to secure impartiality by the use of the ballot, was observed until 1786. The electors' choice was limited, since only aldermen were eligible, and only those who had not served as Mayor for six years past. Moreover, when the eligibles refused to serve there were difficulties. Thus in 1643 five successive elections were made and the Mayor was not duly installed until 10 November; in 1781 three aldermen in turn refused to serve; whilst in 1778 John Forlow was made alderman and Mayor all on one day.

The position of the aldermen, just defined in the ordinance of 1566, grew steadily more assured. In 1581 it was provided that the Mayor might not propound anything to the house without first getting the consent of the aldermen present. In 1599 the power to appoint and remove common councillors was reserved exclusively to the Mayor and aldermen. The 'benchers', apparently senior common councillors recognized as a distinct row in 1572 and 1589, disappear, and the number of aldermen is limited to thirteen including the Mayor.

In 1624, as the electors to the mayoralty had exercised the power given to them in 1572 of electing aldermen as well as town officers, an appeal was made to the Privy Council, which produced the ruling that, in accordance with established usage, only the aldermen could elect aldermen; that no alderman could claim the right of veto or quorum by virtue of seniority; and that none but aldermen could be elected Mayor. Orders drafted in 1629 by a town committee assisted by the Recorder, Talbot Pepys, and the High Steward, Lord Keeper Coventry, laid down that only common councillors could normally be elected aldermen, that normally aldermen should be elected to the Mayoralty 'in due turn', according to seniority; that an alderman refusing to serve should be fined £40; that before any Called Common Day the Mayor should discuss with the aldermen all matters to be proposed and propose nothing without the consent of the majority.

The charter of 1632, the first to mention aldermen and prescribe their number, was only registering their established status when it called them 'the privy council of the Borough'. Nor could the common council limit the aldermen's choice; Lord Keeper Coventry warned the Twenty-Four that if they refused to eject their 'decayed' members in favour of 'abler' men, the aldermen were free to elect any burgess to the bench, as they did in 1655, when four common councillors in turn had refused the aldermanry.

It might indeed be an expensive matter to be an alderman in the 16th or 17th century. From 1558 the wearing of murrey gowns and tippets was prescribed; in 1560 a 20*s*. fine was imposed on all Mayors and ex-Mayors who failed to wear a scarlet gown on the feast days and holidays; whilst the orders of 1575 not only laid down that every alderman should have both murrey and scarlet gowns, but that he should be attended to church by 'at least' one servant.

Samuel Newton's diary, covering the years 1660–1717, gives an admirable picture of the civic career of a leading Cambridge burgess. A freeman by purchase in 1661, he served as treasurer 1664–5, was elected common councillor 1667, alderman 1668, and Mayor 1671. He was a justice of the peace under Charles II, James II, William and Mary, and Anne. He was one of the members of the Corporation removed by James II in April 1688 and restored in the following October. He served as deputy-Mayor in 1690. His accounts of the annual elections show various instances of reluctance to serve as treasurer or bailiff, with readiness to accept the aldermanry with its perquisites of gifts and dinners, and its liabilities mitigated by the purchase of gowns second hand. For the most part vacancies on the bench were only created by death, though in 1669 an alderman resigned in a huff because he was not elected Mayor.

In the 18th century with the rise of party factions the question of the quorum emerges. The orders of 1686 had provided that at least five aldermen must be present for business to be done at a private Common Day, and at the election inquiry of 1715 a number of common councillors declared that by custom at least six must agree to the admission of a freeman, so that the absence of seven aldermen when the Mayor admitted 36 freemen with a view to the approaching parliamentary election was deliberate and successful obstruction.

It was possible for a measure to be carried in a general Common Day by the Mayor and 31 burgesses against seven aldermen and three burgesses but the rule for the presence and consent of six aldermen when the Mayor's honorary freeman was nominated was upheld until 1780, and the consent of six aldermen to corporation business was only declared superfluous in 1785, as a stage in the establishment of the Mortlock dictatorship. In 1787, when 11 aldermen divided 5 and 6 over the election of an alderman, John Forlow senior by voting twice, once as alderman and once with the Mayor's casting vote, secured a majority, and the courts upheld his right in *Rex v. Francis*. Not only town legislation but the election of freemen and of the aldermen themselves had gone back to the body of freemen, and orders of 1789 assimilated the procedure for electing aldermen to that for electing the Mayor, and repealed all orders obliging the Mayor to be elected from the aldermen only. In 1833 the commissioners found that four of the thirteen aldermen were non-resident.

The eclipse of aldermanic power was correlative to that exaltation of the Mayors for which John Mortlock was responsible. Inherited wealth and native ability enabled this young townsman to exploit the divisions in the Corporation between the 'New' and the 'Old' Party which began to affect municipal politics from 1766 onwards. Mortlock's civic career is the complete antithesis of Newton's. Buying his freedom in 1778 he was elected common councillor in 1780, alderman in 1782 and Mayor, at the age of 30, in 1785, an office which he was to hold thirteen times in all before his death in 1816.

His relations with the parliamentary reformers are dealt with below, but his success in making himself 'master of the town of Cambridge' owed little to outside support. The first sign of the coming revolution was the election of Tunwell of the New Party as Mayor in 1783 in defiance of the by-law which prescribed an interval of six years before re-election. Only four of the thirteen aldermen protested and the King's Bench upheld the election, as well as the by-law permitting re-election to the Mayoralty after one year's interval. By alienating his ally Alderman Purchas Mortlock had restored an equal balance to the Bench and his success in 1785 in repealing the order that required the assent of six aldermen to business was recognized by his opponents as a fatal blow. The next step was the repeal in 1786, in Mortlock's own mayoralty, of the order of 1568 for the election of town officers, and the restoration of the regulations of 1344 as 'the ancient custom of the Borough'. The choice of the two initial electors openly, by the Mayor and the whole body of freemen, instead of by drawing lots, meant that the whole course of the election could be arranged in advance. It amounted, said Whittred in 1818, 'to investing Mr. Mortlock with the absolute power of appointing the Mayor'. He openly from the bench gave 'to the two nominees a list of the eighteen he wished to be selected'. Once again the courts, when appealed to in the case of *Newling v. Francis*, upheld the right of the Corporation to alter its own constitution and the ascendancy of Mortlock was established. Between 1784 and 1835 only members of Mortlock's family or faction were Mayors of Cambridge, and all the resources of the Corporation were in his control until his death. His two sons took turns with him from 1801 to 1816 'we called it the bucket system' said a witness in 1833.

It is interesting to note that Mortlock, like his predecessors Hervey fitz Eustace and Roger of Harleston, had extensive landed interests in the county, and that his grandfather had come to Cambridge from Pampisford.

Common Council

An entry in the Cross Book dated 1426 declares that 'from all time of which the memory of man is not to the contrary the Mayor for the time being and twenty-four burgesses . . . to this elected . . . have been accustomed and used to . . . order and determine for the whole rule and government of the town of Cambridge'. Actually the first mention of the Twenty-Four is fifty years earlier; an ordinance of 1376 about the farming of Sturbridge Chapel empowered the Four and Twenty to disfranchise any burgess convicted before them of infringing it. An undated regulation assigned by Cooper to the following year is described as being 'ordained by the Twenty-Four lately elected in the name of the whole commonalty, many of the commonalty being there present'. It is not necessary to interpret the expression 'lately elected' in 1377 as meaning 'set up recently for the first time'. In 1426 also the Twenty-Four had been 'lately elected': they resigned as a body at the Hockday assembly of that year so that a new election might be held. But other towns besides Cambridge had been electing councils of 24 well before 1376.

A council of 24 *electi pro communitate* had appeared in Leicester in 1273, in Yarmouth in 1272, in Norwich about 1308, and in King's Lynn in 1324. Cambridge was in close contact with the last two and was obviously influenced by the customs of Norwich. It is not unreasonable, therefore, to suggest that it was in the first half of the 14th century that the practice began of devolving some of the functions of the Cambridge town assembly upon a smaller group. The town records are too fragmentary for their silence to be conclusive.

Though given judicial powers in 1376, and regarded in 1426 as sharing the executive responsibilities of the Mayor, the Four and Twenty are mostly mentioned in relation to legislation. But in the town records we hear much more about their appointment than about their functions. The 'usual method' in 1426 was for the Mayor and 'his assessors' to elect one man, and the commonalty another, those two to elect eight, who should elect eight more, and the sixteen to elect eight more, making the twenty-four. These were to hold office until death or incapacity, and vacancies so created were to be filled by co-optation. In 1426 it would seem that for the time being the Common Council became a close body. Of those then elected, fourteen had already served as Mayors or Members of Parliament, and four were to do so later. They belong to the inner ring of influential burgesses.

As we have seen, the emergence of the bench of aldermen is an obscure process, and it seems likely that as their status became definite and their number fixed, the importance of the Four and Twenty declined. They are not mentioned between 1426 and 1543, and in 1543 a 'council' distinct from them was assisting the Mayor. They were in process of becoming a pool from which the aldermen were chosen; to be one of the Twenty-Four was to be on the line of advancement to the mayoralty, and it was presumably the competition for that standing that produced the many regulations about election and tenure in the 16th and 17th centuries. In 1546, at the Common Day for electing the Mayor and the other officers, an election of all the Four and Twenty was held; this time no ex-Mayors were chosen, and only eight future Mayors. Six years later a similar election was held; fourteen of those chosen in 1546 were re-elected, and of the ten new-comers seven were future Mayors.

The name 'Comon Counsell' is coming into use for the Four and Twenty, though the old term is not extinct. In 1571 the town assembly ordained that only ex-bailiffs could be chosen to the Twenty-Four. In 1599 by common assent all previous legislation on the subject was repealed, and 'for the avoiding of many inconveniences and abuses committed by the four and twenty', the election was henceforth to be by the Mayor and aldermen only, who might also remove any common councillor at will. The Mayor and ten aldermen 'going together into the parlour' chose twenty-four persons, six of whom ultimately reached the mayoralty. The Mayor's 'privy council' was to have control over the Common Council. But in 1608 the Twenty-Four were given power to fill vacancies in their own body.

In 1629 the orders drafted by the Recorder, Lord Coventry, confirmed this, and provided further that though only the aldermen could elect aldermen, they must choose them from among the Twenty-Four unless the Twenty-Four agreed to the choice of an outsider. The charter of 1632 placed the Common Council firmly in the Borough constitution, but defined neither the method of electing them nor their functions beyond the general statement that they should be helpers and assisters of the Mayor and aldermen whensoever called upon, as of old time.

The bench naturally took a lively interest in elections which would limit their own choice of their fellow aldermen, and in 1654, having failed to induce the Common Council to reject a newly elected councillor, they declared him ejected by vote of the whole assembly, and carried an order that henceforth when a vacancy occurred among the Twenty-Four, they should propose two names between which the common councillor should choose. Though this order was soon repealed, the Mayor in 1699 secured the casting vote in case of a tie. In January 1787, when P. Beales was elected to the Common Council by thirteen votes to nine, the Mayor refused to accept him as having failed to pass the sacramental test, enforced in 1699 but more recently ignored. Next August an order was passed providing that only those who had served the office of treasurer or bailiff were eligible, a condition that Beales had not fulfilled. The courts upheld this second rejection, though not accepting the Mayor's appointment of the defeated candidate. These manœuvres, part of the campaign for establishing the ascendancy of John Mortlock, resulted in two more alterations in the method of electing common councillors. On 29 September 1787 the Corporation passed a by-law that the Common Council should be chosen by the electors of the Mayor and bailiffs. On 17 August 1789 they passed another giving the election to the whole body of freemen. In September, however, they once more assimilated the election of common councillors to that of the Mayor, now returned to the medieval method, and this was retained until 1833.

Freemen

From 1185 it is to the burgesses of Cambridge that grants are made, and not until 1605 does the official style of the Corporation become the Mayor, Bailiffs, and Burgesses. What made a man a burgess, however, is uncertain. Perhaps in 1086 those who held a *masura*, or those who paid hawgavel and land gavel were burgesses; these can be identified in the survey of 1279. Again, it is probable that when John granted the guild merchant in 1201 he was recognizing the existing community of traders, who were thus enabled to admit whom they chose to share the exclusive privileges of the Borough. Hervey, the first Mayor, may have been the alderman of the guild, the name

Guildhall was used for the chief civic building, and the burgesses claimed in 1383 to hold 'their court of the guild merchant, concerning their merchandises, from day to day'.

Apart from that the guild merchant seems to have left no trace on Borough institutions until it was abruptly revived as a dining club in 1547. This may have been the result of studying old charters; in any case it reappeared only to disappear again after 1639. But whatever the nomenclature, undoubtedly the burgess or freeman of Cambridge is the man entitled to practise a trade there without paying toll. This privilege was still 'most desirable' in 1833, when the municipal commissioners were told that the freedom of the Borough might be acquired by birth, by apprenticeship, by purchase, or by gift four categories which had been distinguished at least as early as 1500.

The freeman's oath on admission pledged him to uphold the liberties and customs of the town, to preserve intact its commons and pastures, not to divulge the town's counsel, to obey the Mayor, not to colour the goods of foreigners to deceive the collectors of toll, not to bring a plea in any other court that could be determined before the Mayor and burgesses, and to report the presence of thieves to the town officer.

It is not possible to say what proportion of the inhabitants of the Borough were freemen in the early days. The roll of the court of the liberty for 1294–5 records the admission of eight freemen in twelve months. The receipts from men taking up their liberties in 1347 were £5 16s. 0d., whilst in 1424, £12 13s. 4d. were paid for the admission of fifteen men. But the fees varied according to circumstances. In 1294 they ranged from ½ mark to 2 marks; the first ordinance on the subject, in 1424, provides that the sons of freemen pay 'the old fine' of 3s. 4d. if admitted on their father's death, 6s. 8d. if they take up their freedom in his lifetime. '

Foreigners' paid a heavier fee than natives, and had to secure two resident burgesses as 'godfathers' if they wished their sons to be admitted . The burgess who had an apprentice was made responsible in 1561 for bringing him to the Guildhall on a Common Day to see that he got his freedom before his term was up. In 1534 the Mayor is described as calling all the foreigners in the town to the Guildhall and exhorting them 'to become freemen of the town, and they should be heartily welcome, affirming they had as good a corporation as London had'. This suggests that the freedom was not then in great demand, as does the reduction of entrance fees for burgesses' sons in 1544 and 1576; somewhat surprising, seeing that the freedom carried with it, since 1403, the right to a booth in Sturbridge Fair rent free. But it was noted in 1622 that the expenses of holding office and the financial penalties for refusing to hold office were causing many 'to forbear to be of the Corporation, and many being of the Corporation to forsake it'. Though it cannot be proved, it looks as if the number of Cambridge residents who were freemen was diminishing before any deliberate policy of restriction is traceable.

Apart from the enfranchisement of James of Granchester and his brother in 1381, the practice of bestowing the freedom as a gift on outsiders seems to begin with the making of William Alyngton a freeman for his good and wise counsel by common assent of the whole assembly, on 23 August 1474. In 1568 five country gentlemen, including Sir Giles Alyngton and Lord North, were made freemen so that they might assist in the revision of the election regulations, as one of the town counsel had been in 1566. In 1572 Lord North's eldest son was made a free burgess, and this was apparently regarded as qualifying him to represent the town in Parliament in 1581, in spite of the ordinance requiring residence for the parliamentary burgess. The increasing importance of the House of Commons was affecting the significance of the freedom.

In 1620 Thomas Meautys, in 1625 John Thompson, both London residents, were sworn freemen so that they might be Borough members of Parliament. In January 1640 Oliver Cromwell was admitted to the freedom almost certainly with a view to his election to Parliament in the following March. In 1660 the defeated candidates in the county election were made freemen and elected as town members to the Convention Parliament. Newton's diary gives a picture of the ordinary, unpolitical burgess; he bought his freedom for £6 5s.

in 1661, his immediate object being to secure booths in Sturbridge Fair, though in his 90 years he served a succession of Borough offices. He tells of both apprentices and sons of freemen taking up their freedoms, and mentions the new custom whereby the Mayor could nominate one freeman during his term of office, but he also mentions the admission of several country gentlemen as honorary freemen, one of them as a preliminary to being sworn Recorder of Cambridge.

He does not mention the creation in August 1679 of 22 honorary freemen, mostly country gentlemen, almost certainly in connexion with the Exclusion Bill agitations, though the election had taken place in February. This was the first of many such creations. George Pryme, writing in 1823, supposed that admissions by right of birth were extensive in the first half of the 17th century and that 'the closing of the borough' began about 1680. However that may be, from about that time the freedom of Cambridge, though still retaining some economic significance, was growing steadily more important as conferring the municipal and parliamentary franchise. Non-resident freemen were created to secure new parliamentary electors of the desired complexion, and as factions developed within the Borough, the process of admitting townsmen or outsiders to the small group of residents who controlled Borough government was jealously scrutinized.

In 1688 the Corporation, just 'regulated' by James II, first rescinded the ordinance that fixed the freedom fine for foreigners at £10, and then, under the guidance of their High Steward, James's nominee, Lord Dover of Cheveley, granted the freedom to 150 persons, 65 of them non-resident, in preparation for the expected general election. The Revolution undid this, but the precedent of 1679 had been strengthened. From 1706 the practice became common, and the investigations of the Committee of Privileges in 1710 and 1715, though they exposed the scandal, did not end it.

Various attempts were made to control it. By established custom a freeman could only be admitted in the presence of the Mayor and six aldermen, and it was further provided in 1766 that a freeman must be proposed at one Common Day for election at the next. In 1770 the entrance fee for purchasers was put up to £21, so that in 1782 and again in 1784 the election of a number of honorary freemen was justified as a means of reducing the debt on the new Guildhall. On this occasion each paid 30 guineas.

As the Corporation split into factions the ill-observance of the rule of 1766 led to a number of disputes and lawsuits. Only three of the sixteen freemen admitted three days before the election of 1774 were allowed to vote in it, and these were not numerous enough to defeat the Hardwicke candidate, Soame Jenyns. His correspondence with Hardwicke in 1777 shows that the creation of honorary freemen was a normal procedure, frankly canvassed by Parliamentary candidates. In 1781 when the Hardwicke interest was losing ground he wrote that unless 'a very large number of honorary freemen' was created, it would be better to leave them entirely to themselves.

'It seems to me impracticable without a much greater expense and more trouble than the thing is worth.' In 1784 Ewin expressed the wish that 100 instead of 24 had been created. From 1788 the control both of the Corporation and of the parliamentary seat was secured to the Mortlock-Rutland party. The one limit to their power was the fact, established by *Foster's Case* in 1787, that a freedom once granted could not be revoked.

There was no contested election to Parliament between 1788 and 1818, and, for municipal politics, the existence of a reserve of some 80 non-residents who could be called up at need made contests a foregone conclusion. There were recurrent protests against the withholding of the freedom from freemen's sons, and in 1818 William Whittred attempted to vindicate his right in the King's Bench, but died before his case was tried. Other instances were reported to the commissioners in 1833, when it appeared that, through the obstacles placed in the way of those who were entitled by birth to the freedom, the number of eligible freemen's sons had by that year dwindled to five.

James II's agents had reported in 1688 that there were about 400 electors for Cambridge town. From the poll-books it appears that in 1715 over 300 freemen voted. In 1736, 246 freemen voted, in 1774, 152, of whom 69 were non-resident. In 1783 in a population of 7,000, with 1,200 rate-payers, there were 100 resident and 80 nonresident freemen. In 1833 the number of resident freemen was 118. The artificial character of the freedom is brought out by the fact that, in the county election of 1780, of the 152 men who were qualified to vote by their freeholds in the Borough, only 20 were freemen of the Borough.

Town Assembly or Common Hall

If we pass from the rights of the individual freeman to the freemen acting as a community, we are once more in the dark as to origins. The Borough moot probably long served both judicial and legislative purposes. The earliest record of the town court records the election of the Mayor and the admission of freemen, but the election did not take place on a court day. The transfers of land are witnessed by many other burgesses besides the Mayor and bailiffs, but the early deeds are not dated, so that one cannot be certain at what session they were published. In 1467 a payment is made *in plena curia, coram communitate*, and as late as 1715 a burgess uses the expression 'The Common Day Court'.

Only with the recording of ordinances from 1348 do we begin to make contact with the full assembly of burgesses 'the whole community'. In 1426 we read of 'a colloquy and treaty' between the Mayor and the burgesses, also called a 'congregation', and in 1460 the Hock Tuesday assembly is described as 'the great congregation of burgesses'. This wording indicates that by that date certain days were appropriated to specially full meetings of the burgesses. Three of these were certainly established at an early date: Michaelmas, when the Mayor-elect was sworn in, 9 September, the day of election, and Hock Tuesday, the day for electing the treasurers. In an ordinance of 1499 in which the term 'Common Day' first occurs, the Tuesday after Epiphany figures as an annual occasion.

The records of the assembly used by Cooper began in 1544; he cites an ordinance made in 1556 which distinguished between 'special' and 'general' Common Days, and in 1624 it was declared specifically, as there had been some question about it, that the five general Common Days were Michaelmas, Tuesday after Twelfth Night, Hock Tuesday, election day, and Bartholomew Day. These are the 'Grand Common Days' of the 17th and 18th centuries; the term 'charter days' used in 1833 has no warrant by fact or usage.

They do not seem to have any relation to the five court days named by the burgesses in 1383, nor to the five terms for accounting kept by the Mayor and bailiffs. The other Common Halls were either adjournments or 'special' or 'Called Common Days' summoned by the Mayor at his discretion, recognized in the charter of 1632. James I had acknowledged the right of the Mayor and burgesses to make by-laws; Charles I specified that such laws should be made by the Mayor, bailiffs, and burgesses, 'gathered and assembled for this purpose, on a public summons by the Mayor'.

During the parliamentary inquiry into the election of 1715 a very full statement was made regarding the customary method of holding Common Days. The five general Common Days are said to be fixed by charter. The private or summoned Common Days are held when the Mayor thinks fit, one day's notice at least being the rule. Freemen should only be admitted at a General Common Day, or at a summoned Common Day at which at least six aldermen are present. Precedents going back to 1554 are cited.

The Common Day Books give a wealth of information about the business done in Common Hall in the 16th, 17th, and 18th centuries. Besides the passing of ordinances or by-laws, and the annual elections of officials at Hocktide and mid-August there are occasional elections, as of the Recorder, the High Steward, the Town Clerk and the burgesses for Parliament, either by a committee or by the majority of all the burgesses. Authority is given to a delegation to act for the Corporation in some matter; leases or exchanges of Corporation property are authorized and repairs or improvements ordered;

arrangements are made in connexion with civic feasts, with Sturbridge Fair or with royal visits; letters from noble friends and patrons are read and acted upon; petitions or loyal addresses to the Crown are approved.

The development first of the Common Council and then of the bench of aldermen reduced the powers and activity of the assembly, especially after the presence of six aldermen was made necessary for the transaction of business in Common Hall. Newton describes how at Michaelmas 1668 'The Mayor and aldermen going first into the parlour and propounding and considering what was fit to be propounded at the Common Day, within a quarter of an hour went into the Hall, and the Common Day being opened, there was propounded what in the parlour was thought fit to be propounded'. But though policy might be determined by the 'private council' of the Mayor and his brethren, legislation required the assent of the commonalty, and the Common Days were held regularly until 1835.

After the by-law dispensing with the assent of six aldermen was passed in 1785, so many of the losing faction stayed away that for a few months in 1787 fines for absence were imposed, which evoked from old alderman Whittred the protest that 'he knew no use in the Common Days'. They were indeed coming to do little more than register the edicts of a dictator. By a paradox it was the nominal revival of the powers of the body of freemen by the restoration of direct election in the years 1785–9 that, along with the *ad hoc* creation of freemen and the reduction of their numbers, finally discredited the town assembly. Whatever powers were given to the townsmen by municipal reform, the Common Days ceased after 1835.

The order of sitting at the Common Days as laid down in 1787 gives a picture of the *ordo dignationum* in unreformed Cambridge. The bench with the Mayor and other aldermen was above the table, at which none but the Town Clerk ought to sit; below the table sat first the 24 Common Councillors, then the 'dispensers', that is, those who had fined to be dispensed from serving as bailiffs or treasurers, in the order in which they had obtained dispensation and thus become eligible to be common council men; and below them the freemen or burgesses. The whole body of those below the table constituted 'the floor'. In 1833 the average number attending the meetings of the Corporation was 33, in a body of 118 resident freemen.

Town Courts

At least from the time when the shire of Cambridge was constituted with fifteen hundreds, of which Cambridge Borough was reckoned one, there must have been a Borough court of status similar to that of the rural hundreds. To the Danish occupation may be traced the lawmen of Domesday book, who are to be equated probably with the 24 *judices* of the *Liber Eliensis*. The *Liber* records that a number of legal transactions concerning land transfers and stolen merchandise took place at Cambridge *coram tota civitate* or *coram coetu civium*, and testifies to a well-established local custom 'that pledges were not needed when land was purchased at Cambridge, any more than at Norwich, Thetford, and Ipswich'. A Borough court then had presumably been in existence for some 150 years when the writ of 1118 recognized its jurisdiction over offences committed within the Borough.

In 1201 John further recognized the burgesses' right to a defence in pleas of the Crown 'according to the ancient custom of the Borough'. No Cambridge custumal is extant; the only customs specifically recorded are the right of a person to devise his church to a relative, already obsolete in 1207; the right of a landlord to distrain on the whole holding for arrears of rent; and the right of a widow to half her husband's chattels on his death. Henry III in 1256 recognized the right to hold pleas of replevin, and the 13th-century records show the town courts hearing pleas of dower, land, nuisance, trespass, debt, covenant, account, quittance, distraint and assault, petty larceny, and grand larceny, and taking proceedings preliminary to the hearing of pleas before the king's justices. In the eyre of January 1261 a plea between two townsmen for a house was referred back to the town court, since the writ *pone* could not apply.

In the same eyre a widow claiming dower failed in her plea because her husband had formerly lost the land by judgement of the court of Cambridge, and the rolls of the said court were searched for the names of pledges. In the seventeen courts held for the year 1295-6 thirteen people were convicted of larceny and ten were hanged. It appears that the competence and procedure of the Cambridge courts matched those of Norwich, where manifest theft at the suit of a party could be dealt with before the coroner and a bailiff whilst appeals of felony went to the county court, and other forms of larceny were reserved for the justices of gaol delivery. As larceny came to be classed as a felony, the town court would lose such cases.

Transfers of land took place in the court before the Mayor and bailiffs, and many fines made there are extant, the earliest reference to a chirograph 'made in the town court before many men of the town' belonging probably to the year 1220. A transfer made in another county is formally recorded there about 1268. In 1286, according to the Barnwell chronicler, a quitclaim to the prior was declared invalid because made before the Mayor and bailiffs and not before the justices who bear record, but the number of surviving deeds goes to show that very many Cambridge burgesses found the record of the Mayor's court adequate for their land transactions in the 13th and 14th centuries.

Other business done in the medieval town courts was the proving of wills, the swearing in of freemen, and the acknowledgement of debts.

Like other boroughs, Cambridge had different courts for the exercise of its different jurisdictions. In 1383, in making a claim of cognizance in the King's Bench, then sitting at Cambridge, the Mayor and bailiffs of Cambridge enumerated the courts held in the town under the royal charters, 1207–1313, as follows: The *prepositus* and bailiffs hold their court concerning lands and tenements on five Mondays in the year those after St. Matthew's, St. Lucy's, Mid-lent, Trinity and St. James's. They also hold a weekly court on Tuesdays for trespasses and for contracts and covenants made within the town. Thirdly they hold pleas of trespass and so forth in which 'foreigners' are concerned 'from day to day' as occasion demands. Fourthly they hold their court of the guild merchant between merchants concerning their merchandise, and lastly they hold courts at Easter and Michaelmas for leet business and view of frankpledge. Two ordinances in the *Cross Book* describe the court held on Mondays as the Court of the Liberty. Cooper cites that of 1405 which provides that surrenders of booths in Sturbridge Fair may be made by burgesses in either the Monday or the Tuesday court; he omits that of 1424, which is as follows:

It is ordained by the Four and Twenty, on Tuesday after St. Gregory's in the second year of King Henry VI, in the Guild Hall of the town of Cambridge, in the presence of many of the community of the said town, by the advice of John Burgoyne, William Gudred and Nicholas Hywyssh there present, that any burgess impleaded on any Tuesday in the court of the Mayor and bailiffs claim to have his franchise and to be assigned to the court of the liberty held on Mondays every three weeks and have nothing whereby he can be distrained for the said plea, that [sic] straightway the process shall be continued before the said Mayor and bailiffs up to the end of the said plea, and the said defendant shall then find sufficient manucaptors there in the presence of the Mayor and bailiffs that he will answer to the said plaintiff in the aforesaid court of the liberty according to the law and custom of the said vill.

From this it appears that the weekly court was for all and sundry and the three-weekly court of the liberty for freemen of the Borough. Its roll for 1294–5 survives, and records sessions on every third Monday of the year, but it would seem that like other contemporary courts it continued to be described as 'three-weekly' long after it met normally only five times a year. There is no unequivocal reference to it after 1424, and no later rolls are extant, for the scanty records of the 'court of the town of Cambridge held at the Guildhall before the Mayor and bailiffs' in the years 1314–16 relate to courts held on Mondays, Tuesdays, Wednesdays, and Saturdays at irregular intervals, from a week upwards, and are presumably the 'day to day' sessions for civil pleas between townsmen and strangers.

If the three-weekly court of the liberty disappeared, there is ample evidence of the survival of the weekly court, which probably absorbed its jurisdiction. A surviving court book for 1389–90 records fairly regular Tuesday sessions at which pleas of debt, covenant, detinue, account, and trespass are heard and merchants from London, Northampton, and Bury St. Edmunds as well as men from the Cambridgeshire villages appear as litigants. Annotations with initials probably denote the names of the four bailiffs, each responsible for execution in his own ward, and the entries are crossed through, indicating that the requisite action has been taken.

An ordinance of 1403 forbade burgesses to prosecute in any other court contracts which could be determined before the Mayor and bailiffs, on pain of disfranchisement, and the enforcement of this penalty against two burgesses in 1578 no less than the various ordinances from 1499 to 1692 regulating the number and the fees of the attorneys practising in the town court, are evidence of its activity. Newton, when treasurer in 1664, noted that 21 causes were heard on one day, and Tuesday is 'court day' for him, as it had been in 1609 and 1594.

In 1650 and again in 1658 the Mayor and bailiffs claimed cognizance of all pleas and tenements within the town, as well as of trespass, covenants, and contracts, but apart from occasional fines and transfers of booths in Sturbridge Fair its jurisdiction had probably shrunk to personal actions merely long before 1833. A court book for the years 1724–36, which incidentally registers the transition from Latin to English in recording pleas, shows the court meeting always on Tuesdays, at intervals ranging from one to five weeks, and handling pleas of debt, trespass, and assault. It is described as 'The court of pleas of our sovereign lord the king for the town of Cambridge held in the Guildhall of the same town before Mayor and and bailiffs.' In 1833 the municipal commissioners were told that it met once a month on Tuesdays; that though two bailiffs attended, the Mayor was the sole judge; that its jurisdiction was in practice limited to personal actions, most of which were settled by agreement.

Of the 68 cases brought before it in the last three years, none had come to an issue for trial. It had no very good reputation, as the Mayors knew no law, and apart from suspicions of political bias, the processes were cumbrous and expensive. Under the Municipal Corporations Act of 1835 the Recorder replaced the Mayor as judge of the town court, 3 bailiffs attending for execution of process and the Town Clerk being registrar. Between 1837 and 1839 the court entertained 418 pleas, but only 59 were brought to execution. In February 1840 1,400 Cambridge inhabitants signed a petition for the establishment of a court for the recovery of small debts. Under the County Courts Act of 1846 such a court was set up for Cambridge and the surrounding region, and the last *raison d'être* for the old Court of Record disappeared, though it was never formally abolished.

Few records are extant of proceedings between merchant and merchant in the Pie Powder courts, but those arising in Reach Fair in 1508 have been preserved and include actions of debt and deceit. A court house for the Mayor was erected at Sturbridge in 1654 and pulled down in 1802.

Nor do many records survive of the October and April leets mentioned in 1383. By an ordinance of 1374 all burgesses had to attend on pain of money penalties and the forfeiture of freedom for the third default, and Metcalfe mentions a tradition that they had to be kept 'in the field' because the numbers were so great. The petty criminal jurisdiction of the court was absorbed, here as elsewhere, after 1461 by the justices of the peace, but it was still active in presenting nuisances and upholding peace measures. In 1502 266 persons were charged with nuisances or purprestures; and in the spring leet of 1561 59 apprentices were enrolled in the queen's tithing and 28 foreigners took the oath of allegiance to the queen.

From 1459 the University, with its concurrent responsibility for town hygiene, held its own leet, swearing in a jury of townsmen and by the 1503 indenture it could take action if the Mayor failed to do so within six weeks. The Paving Act of 1544 added a paving leet, held jointly by Vice-Chancellor and Mayor twice a year. Newton's account in 1664 shows that there were two distinct juries, but the amercements which the treasurers collected, amounting to £3 10*s*., seem to have arisen in the paving leet. The leets were still being held in 1733, but the paving leet must have been extinguished by the Paving Act of 1788. A petition of 1790 relating to a dunghill is directed to a 'court' which was presumably the leet of nuisances, but in 1833 the commissioners were told that the court leet had ceased to assemble some fifteen or twenty years before.

Justices of the Peace

The first recorded commission of the peace for the Borough was issued to the Mayor and bailiffs in 1344. Another was issued in May 1380 which included both the Mayor and the Vice-Chancellor, but in September 1380 a separate commission for enforcing peace in the University was issued and the Mayor and his fellows were warned not to intermeddle with the masters. In February 1381 the Mayor was bound over to keep the peace as a result of obstructing the holding of the town sessions, and his name does not appear with that of the Vice-Chancellor on the commission issued after the rising. All town commissions were revoked on 9 December 1381 and no further ones issued until 1392. Thenceforward the name of the Mayor appears in every extant commission for the Borough. The fact that the Vice-Chancellor and other members of the University were invariably also on the commission explains why there was in Cambridge no such merger of the traditional town jurisdictions with the sessions of the peace as occurred frequently elsewhere.

A picture of the activities of Cambridge justices of the peace in the 17th century is given in the note-books of Sir Thomas Sclater, M.D., Fellow of Trinity, freeman of the Borough from 1670, and member of both town and county commissions of the peace from 1661 to 1684. He issued warrants for apprehending vagrants and runaway apprentices, receivers of stolen goods, breakers of windows, robbers of orchards and fishponds; he supervised the swearing-in of constables and the accounts of collectors of excise and hearth money; he broke up conventicles and inquired into seditious speeches. His eight or nine colleagues at quarter sessions were mainly aldermen, but Dr. Stoyt of the University was very active.

In 1664 the charge was given by the Recorder, Roger Pepys, and the business was finished in one day. Though the justices had to deal with burglary, arson and sedition, bastardy and apprenticeship cases and the regulation of the spittle house recur more frequently. Sir Thomas's note on a quarrel between neighbours in 1665 'I made them all friends' is thoroughly in keeping with the tone of his record. The commission of 1682 among its nineteen members included several other county gentlemen besides the borough members of Parliament. The political motive in naming the commission comes out in a letter of S. Shepheard the elder to Harley in August 1710: '

According to your command I send the names of the justices of the peace turned out at Cambridge upon my son being chosen for that place T. Ewin, F. Fox Senior, C. Chambers Senior and T. Fowler, all aldermen of the town.' Of the four who replaced them, only one was a Cambridge resident. Two generations later another Ewin, like Sclater a member of the University, a resident of the town and a justice for both town and county, reported on the sessions to Lord Hardwicke. For all his Borough ancestry, his sympathies were closest with the county gentry, but whether honestly or from sycophancy he represented the Borough as the natural field for county ambitions. He quoted Keene, the town member, as saying in 1780: 'I don't care a farthing what they do in the county; I am only concerned with the town.'

Upon this his comment was: 'It was enough to judge how little he cared about matters.' In 1776 he described how two vagrants were induced to enlist very promptly by the sentence, as an alternative, of three floggings and three months in prison. When in 1778 he fell into disgrace for lending money to undergraduates at an extortionate rate he resented bitterly the attempt of the University to have him put out of the commission, and succeeded in getting both his town and county colleagues to protest against his removal. The Lord Chancellor's refusal to put him in the new commission of 1781 he considered 'vindictive conduct'.

Though collaboration between the town and the University justices of the peace seems to have been easy in the days of Sclater and Ewin, on occasion the sessions of the peace proved yet one more field of rivalry between town and gown. Precedence on the bench was a recurrent issue from 1596, when the University was greatly offended at the Mayor's name being placed first in the Commission, until 1818, when the ViceChancellor acquiesced peaceably in John Purchas's 'positive and unequivocal' refusal to surrender the seat he occupied as chairman of the commission. Since 1836 the ViceChancellor has as a rule been appointed justice of the peace for the town along with the Mayor.

Town Clerk

The existence of rolls of the town court in 1261 implies that the town then had a clerk, but no certain identification is found before William of Harwood, whose fee of 6s. 8d. is entered on the treasurers' roll for 1346–7. In 1418 Richard Parys was mentioned as common clerk of the town. The records of the subsidy of 1512 named John Thyrleby as Town Clerk of Cambridge and assessed the profits of his office as between £2 and £10; in 1514 he was paid 7s. 4d. for writing the treasurers' roll and for parchment.

He was still in office in 1531, and very likely until his death in 1539. In 1545 it was provided that the Recorder might not appoint a town clerk without the consent of the town; and all the evidence goes to show that he was thenceforth elected in Common Day. It would seem that the tenure was already for life, since Edward Ball, who had to apologize to the Vice-Chancellor in 1583 for abusing the University to the Lord Mayor of London at Sturbridge Fair, served from 1557 to 1596, when he resigned his office. His Register Book is still in the City archives. The office was apparently a profitable one. When Ball's successor Henry Slegge died in 1629, King Charles himself urged the appointment of Roger Slegge 'trayned up by the space of twenty years in hope that he should succeed his father'.

The Corporation had, however, granted the reversion of the office to North Harrison in 1610 for life, at £5 a year, with fees and emoluments, and though Roger Slegge was elected, he had, by a decree of Lord Keeper Coventry, to hand over the office and the books to Harrison a year later. In January 1632 Harrison's son, John, was granted the office for which his father had had to wait so long, on the same terms, and held it until his death in 1660, but once again a claimant was waiting for the dead man's shoes, for Alderman Samuel Spalding had been granted the reversion in 1637, and held it from the age of 70 for nine years only. From the time of the Slegges the office would seem to have been the object of aldermanic rivalry.

The most sensational episode occurred in 1707 when Joseph Pyke, who had hoped to succeed his father as Town Clerk, was stabbed in the Rose Tavern by Alderman Thomas Fox the younger, who obtained the position by a majority of 40. From 1731 to 1756 the office was held by two ex-Mayors, Syndrey and York, but in 1745 the Corporation ordered that for the future no alderman should be chosen Town Clerk. James Day, common councillor and Town Clerk from 1756 to 1788, was, however, as deeply involved in town politics as any alderman.

He was one of the most ardent supporters of 'the old interest', and is mentioned more than once in the Hardwicke correspondence as a regular reporter of Cambridge news. His sins as custodian of the town records are only excelled by those of York, through whose slackness the treasurers' rolls found their way to the church chest of St. Michael's and were only saved from imminent destruction by Bowtell. During the last year of his term of office James Day was being constantly ordered to produce town books in connexion with the numerous corporation lawsuits. He was threatened with dismissal for refusing to produce them, and on his resignation a committee was appointed to draw up an inventory.

One at least was retained by him and given by his brother and executor after his death to Bowtell, whilst other valuable records disappeared. A volume of the Common Day Books, long missing, contains an inscription recording its return to the custody of the town. Day's successor, Robert White, elected by the triumphant Mortlock faction at Michaelmas 1788, had the usual life patent, and was succeeded in due course by his son and his grandson to the scandal of the commissioners of 1833.

The duties of the town clerk included keeping the records both of the courts and of the assemblies. In 1557 he was sworn 'to write all orders truly'. It was presumably the fees and perquisites that made it a coveted position. In 1833 the fees averaged £260 a year, and the salary was £40: he was the legal adviser of the Corporation and the post was always held by an attorney.

The greatest of all Cambridge Town Clerks, Charles Henry Cooper, was not a native of the town, but settled there in 1826 and made himself familiar with local antiquities while pursuing his profession as a solicitor. His legal abilities were warmly commended in connexion with the complicated preliminaries to Sir John Patteson's award of 1855. He was elected the first town coroner under the reformed Corporation in 1836, and was Town Clerk from 1849 until his death in 1866, but he was studying the archives well before he became their official custodian, and the first volume of his *Annals of Cambridge* was published in 1843. Four more volumes followed, the last, with an index, being published posthumously in 1908. His *Memorials of Cambridge* and his *Athenae Cantabrigienses* dealt with the buildings and topography of Cambridge and the careers of distinguished graduates; at least as valuable to the student of Cambridge institutions was the report of the Borough Rate Committee, which was printed anonymously in 1850. All who have worked on Cambridge history, from Maitland to W. M. Palmer and Milner Gray, have had reason to appreciate the amazing industry and accuracy of Cooper's work, which remains the starting point for all further discoveries.

Coroners

By the charter of 1256 the burgesses were granted the right to elect their own coroners and five years later in the eyre of 1261 there are several references to the coroner Harvey Parleben. The coroner's rolls are cited, the coroner himself is amerced for dereliction of duty, and one passage suggests that the liberty of choosing coroners might be revoked for failure to attach or exact criminals according to the law of England. Two coroners were named in 1294 and 1299. This was the regular number and later records indicate that they were elected annually.

Henry Hawlehed, elected Mayor in 1514, had served as coroner the previous year. The provisional regulations of 1566 provided that the two youngest aldermen should always serve as coroners, and the ordinance of 1568 prescribed that they should be elected at the same time and in the same way as the Mayor. The coroner's oath is entered in the order book of 1609. On several occasions a coroner elect successfully claimed, as the privilege of an attorney, exemption from serving, but not all put in this plea. In 1833 it was reported that one of the two coroners was usually an attorney; that they were elected annually from the commonalty, but usually re-elected and served for long terms.

Recorder

The first mention of a recorder in Cambridge is in 1494, when John Leynton, who had represented the town in the Parliament of 1489, was paid 6s. 8d. for receiving and determining the treasurers' accounts as 'Recorder and auditor'. Five years later John Woode, 'Recorder of the town of Cambridge', received the same fee for the same service, but he also received £1 6s. 8d. as 'lawyer and of the counsel of the town, for the business of the town and keeping and supporting the rights of the same'. For many years previously the town had been retaining counsel for its business, whether, as in 1418, in a dispute with the University, or, as in 1424 or 1426, for the drafting of ordinances about the town courts or the Common Council, and these services were recognized by hospitality as well as by fees.

In 1500 the Recorder John Woode rode to Huntingdon on town business and gave labour and counsel divers times in the town's dispute with Barnwell Priory about the title to a ditch on Midsummer Common, as well as in the matter between the University and the town. There might be other 'learned counsell' of the town, but the Recorder was, it seems, the senior legal adviser. His functions are well described in the letter in which the Mayor and Corporation declined the queen's offer in 1559 to permit George Frevill to retain the office after becoming a baron of the Exchequer.

According to that letter the Recorder of Cambridge was one 'learned in the lawes of this your Realme, to whome as well the Corporacion of your highnesse said towne, as every particular person of the same, might resort for Counsell as occasyon served, And such a one also as not only might speak in any of your Majesties Courts for such matters as we from time to time have had in sute . . . but also should assist us in the Courts holden within in the said towne, as well for the furtherance of Justice . . . as for the instructing of us, being simple and unlearned men, in doubtfull matters in the lawe'. This, it was implied, was not compatible with serving as a royal justice, and so 'time out of mind' they had been accustomed to choose another Recorder if such advancement occurred. Such skilled advice was especially needful in the later 16th century, when the town was constantly at issue with the University; it was also called for when the town orders were revised in 1609, and Recorder Brackyn and Mr. Weston took great pains in amending them.

But by this date the emphasis was shifting from technical knowledge to social influence; the 'counsel' might be of a political as much as of a legal character. The office had been held by a succession of king's serjeants: John Hynde, William Cooke, George Freville, Robert

Shute. The transition was marked by the departure in 1579 from the principle laid down in 1559. By royal command, Shute was continued as Recorder after he had become baron of the Exchequer; he also represented Cambridge in Parliament from 1572 to 1581. On Shute's death in 1590 the town elected to the post the queen's cousin, Lord Hunsdon, the Lord Chamberlain, whose advocacy would be personal, not professional, and Francis Brackyn, a local lawyer, was appointed as deputy recorder.

From this point onwards the typical Recorder was the noble patron, who seems almost to duplicate the office of the High Steward. Sir Thomas Egerton, indeed, resigned the recordership in 1600 to become High Steward. In 1608 Brackyn who had been deputy under three Recorders became Recorder himself. His successors Talbot and Roger Pepys were, like himself, working lawyers, but in 1679 the régime of the magnates was resumed, and baronets and peers only occasionally make way for commoners. John Mortlock held the office with that of Mayor and Member of Parliament for three months in 1788, passing it on to the Duchess of Rutland's brother, who was succeeded by her two sons. The deputies were professional lawyers until 1835, and were magistrates of the Borough; they received no fee, and their attendance at sessions was not regular. Since 1835 the Recorder has been a professional lawyer and the presiding magistrate at Quarter Sessions.

High Steward

It seems that the first High Steward of the Borough was elected in 1529, shortly after the King's Bench had admitted the claim of the Mayor and burgesses that Cambridge was a Corporation by prescription, a status that carried with it the right to sue or be sued. It may have been in anticipation of other lawsuits that it was deemed advisable to secure the good offices of a noble patron. No earlier institution of a High Stewardship has been noted in any borough. The Duke of Norfolk received his patent under the common seal of the Borough and accepted an annual fee of 40s. He was superseded in the whirligig of politics successively by the Dukes of Somerset and Northumberland, and resumed his office on the death of Edward VI.

His grandson who succeeded him in 1554 was offended at the 'unworthy rejection' of his recommendations in the municipal elections of 1569 and resigned, regardless of the town's ordinance appointing him the only equitable court of appeal in disputes between burgesses not determinable at common law. He was induced to resume the office, however, although the University, afraid, presumably, of his influence as attorney for the town in disputes between them, tried to dissuade him. In 1572 he followed his predecessors to the block, and the town turned to a representative of the new nobility, their neighbour at Kirtling, Roger, Lord North, whose steady friendship and support to the Borough from 1572 to 1600 as its

High Steward evoked the gratitude recorded year by year on the treasurers' rolls in the form of gifts of 'hippocras', 'muscadyns', 'marchpayne', white wine, fish, flocks of wethers, and other 'remembrances', as well as dinners and suppers. His sons, John and Henry, were made freemen and parliamentary representatives of the town in 1581 and 1584 and his impecunious brother, Thomas, was accorded a 'benevolence' of £20 in 1598.

It seems, however, that neither High Steward nor Recorder had their way in the parliamentary elections of 1593 and 1601. From 1600 to 1640 the office was held by four Lord Keepers in succession, Ellesmere, Bacon, Coventry, and Finch, and in the elections of 1614, 1620, 1625, 1626, and March 1640 the town paid the price for patronage by reserving one seat for the High Steward's nominee. The office, more and more honorary, was suspended after Finch's flight to the Continent in December 1640.

Neither Cromwell nor Clarendon concerned themselves particularly with Borough politics, and from 1670 on the High Stewards were country gentlemen or noblemen Chicheley of Wimpole, Russell of Chippenham, Harley of Wimpole, Bromley of Horseheath, and Manners of Cheveley the lords of county politics. It is interesting that the political dominance attributed to Lord Hardwicke by his dependants in the 1770's and 1780's found no reflection in any Borough office; he was Lord Lieutenant of the county, High Steward of the University and President of Addenbrooke's Hospital, but neither High Steward nor Recorder of the Borough.

It was, presumably, during the Interregnum that the High Steward's fee of 40*s*. ceased to be paid; in 1833 the office is described as having neither duties nor emoluments, though the terms of appointment named a salary of £6 13*s*. 4*d*. The title has now become a distinction conferred on outstanding sons of Cambridge such as Macaulay, John Maynard Keynes, and George Macaulay Trevelyan, O.M. The disappearance of one possible reason for its existence was indicated when in 1862 it was conferred on the Chancellor of the University, the seventh Duke of Devonshire.

Town Waits

From the 15th century, Cambridge, like Norwich, Thetford, Lynn, and several other towns, maintained a band of town minstrels or waits. The treasurers' accounts, which frequently enter payments to minstrels accompanying royal and noble visitors to the town, first mention the town minstrels in 1484 when 16*s*. 4*d*. had been spent on their vestments. Similar payments are noted under 1489, 1491, 1494, 1500, and 1501. The livery was generally of sanguine woollen cloth, but once the cheaper tawny is used. They were apparently three in number; in 1511 the Bassingbourn churchwardens' accounts record the payment of 5*s*. 6*d*. to three waits of Cambridge who had accompanied the performances of the play of St. George on their round of the neighbouring parishes. The chief wait, John Martyn, has a fee of £2 and a gown priced 10s. in 1512, and the subsidy records show him to be a man of substance, having movables worth £40 to £100 and with two apprentices.

That the position conferred prestige appears from the provision at a Great Common Day in 1552 that if Bennett Pryme does not wish to continue to be a wait along with John Richemond and John Clerke, they are to co-opt a third minstrel with the approval of the Mayor, the consent of the whole house being needed for any change.

The waits' silver collars are mentioned in 1551 and 1564 when two new ones were made, indicating that their number had been increased to five, probably in view of the queen's visit of that year. Tudor magnificence, it may be conjectured, in this as in other matters, had taxed the resources of the townsmen too heavily: in 1622 it was agreed that the fee to the town waits should cease, but it was restored next year. It had been a retainer rather than a salary; special payments were made on special occasions, such as the celebration of the capture of Edinburgh and Boulogne in 1544, the proclamation of James I's accession in 1603 or the treasurers' feast in 1608, and the visit of the High Steward, Lord Clarendon, in 1664.

They played when the charter of Charles II was read in 1685, when William III visited the town in 1689, and when war was declared on

Spain in 1761. They took part regularly in the Mayor's procession at Sturbridge Fair and it is possible that the discontinuance of that procession in 1790 was the death blow to the official town music. When in 1799 the victory of the Nile was celebrated it was the Band of the Volunteer Associations which paraded the town.

The Cambridge town waits are of more than local interest as being the field of activity of the Gibbons family. In 1567 William Gibbons 'musitian' was appointed leader of the town waits and given charge of their five silver collars. Possibly he had been brought in three years before for Elizabeth I's visit; but he married a Cambridge woman and settled in the town, where eight of his ten children were born, where, in 1576, he was paid by the Vice-Chancellor for keeping a dancing school, and where, in 1574 and 1578, he was a vestryman of Holy Trinity. He was buried there in 1596, but between 1583 and 1588 he was living at Oxford, probably his native town, and served as one of the city waits there. He was a householder and a freeman of Oxford. Thus it was in Oxford that his youngest and most famous son, Orlando, was born and baptized in December 1583; though as the family returned to Cambridge in 1588 Orlando's musical career began with his admission to the choir of King's College Chapel in 1596, and it was at Cambridge that he took his bachelor's degree in music.

Treasurers and Town Revenues

According to Maitland 'the evolution of a borough corporation is very closely connected with the emergence of a freely disposable revenue'. When Cambridge acquired from the Crown the right and duty of collecting the ancient customary dues, rents, and profits of the Borough, there were probably few other profitable assets at the disposal of the burgesses. But in course of time other sources of revenue appeared, and whereas the ancient revenues inherited from the Crown and levied by the bailiffs had small expanding power, these other assets developed considerably. Maitland suggests that 'a steady income of this kind would hardly be found before the fourteenth century in any but the largest towns'. It is, in fact, in 1338 that we meet the first reference to the treasurers, who were responsible for all sources of revenue other than those for which the bailiffs accounted. A town order of that year provided that the penalty for not committing cattle to the common herdman was to be paid half to the Mayor and bailiffs and half to the treasurers for the time being. In the earliest account roll surviving, that of 1347, these officials are also described as 'receivers'. There is nothing to indicate when or why they were instituted, but the borough of Colchester in 1372 set up two receivers or chamberlains to check the lavish spending of the town bailiffs, and it may well be that they were imitating an action taken by Cambridge for similar reasons. At Colchester, as at Cambridge, the office of treasurer was held by men who had not yet served as bailiff, and the term was from September to September. At Cambridge, however, it was customary to elect them on Hock Tuesday although all other elections were held in September.

They were chosen by a method of double election, similar to that used in choosing the Mayor. At first they held office from 9 September to 9 September, but from 1528 onwards they were sworn in at Michaelmas like the Mayor, having to give security in 20 marks. A treasurer was sworn 'to give due attendance upon Mr. Maior and the Counsell of the Towne and truly collect and gather all Rentes resolutes to the Treasury of the Towne due and belonginge and of all the Revenewes and Profittes cominge to your handes by the reason of the sayd office you shall yeeld a true accompt'. In 1590 a fine of £10 was imposed if an elected treasurer refused to serve.

The revised rules of 1622, which provided that the treasurers should not be forced to disburse more than they had received, indicate that the holding of the office might be a financial liability. The charter of 1632, which is the first to mention the treasurers, provides for their annual election and empowers them to sue in the Borough court for money penalties incurred by violators of the by-laws. Samuel Newton, one of the two treasurers for 1664–5, speaks more of the treasurers' perquisites than of their duties. His description of the audit at the Guildhall before three aldermen, three other burgesses and the town clerk, corresponds to the description given to the commissioners in 1833.

By that date all the duties of the treasurers were being performed by the senior treasurer alone; he had ceased to give any security and the audit had become a mere form. His annual election, abandoned between 1787 and 1819, was also a matter of form; he was regularly re-elected unopposed. Well before that date the financial responsibilities of the bailiffs had been finally taken over by the treasurers. The ancient distinction between Crown and town revenues had been finally obliterated and the separate accounts merged in one in 1795.

As we have seen, the ancient Crown revenues, probably from before the Norman Conquest, were made up of haw gavel and land gavel, the tolls and the profits of justice, and it is for these that the bailiffs account at the 'ports'. The first item has a long and remarkable history. Though the two terms used imply a dual origin, the land and house taxes had merged in one by 1086. In Domesday Book the land gavel is said to bring in £7 and 2 *orae* and 2*d*.; the sums payable for 'hagabulum and landgabulum' in 1279 have been calculated to amount to nearly £8; the totals collected under this heading in 1483 and 1491 were £7 10*s*. 5¾*d*. and £7 7*s*. 1*d*. respectively, and a roll for the early 17th century records the payment of £7 2*s*. 10*d*.

It was a permanent charge on particular houses and sites, and items can be traced unchanged for centuries. The distribution of liability is probably a guide to the distribution of inhabited houses before 1066, and when, in the later Middle Ages, houses were destroyed to make way for colleges, the liability was transferred to the colleges. In the 18th century the smallness of the sums levied led to refusal to pay or neglect to levy. But the Corporation still collects 'hagable rents' to the amount of £1 12s. 1d.

The tolls probably included those on waterborne goods landed at the Cambridge hithes under the writ of Henry I, the market tolls, the mill tolls and the through tolls levied on loaded carts and beasts driven through the town. In 1330 the burgesses referred to the market tolls as their main source of revenue and the protest of the University in 1503 against excessive tolls refers to picage, stallage, tolls on victuals brought into the town and hawked in the streets, tolls on livestock, on riverborne grain, and on loaded carts as being levied by old custom. The tolls on carts loaded with building material were particularly irksome when 15th-century building was in progress. As regarded outsiders, there were recurrent disputes from the 13th to the 17th century with the merchants of Lynn, Saffron Walden, Northampton, Bury St. Edmunds, and Huntingdon as to the payment of toll at Cambridge.

From 1279 to 1769 the Corporation also collected the bridge tolls on Whittlesford Bridge, estimated in 1521 to bring in 20s. a year towards the fee farm, of which 6s. 8d. was put aside for a repairing fund. As early as 1499 the bridge tolls were farmed out. In 1769 a farmer paid 5 guineas a year to the Corporation and was responsible for the upkeep of the bridge, but by the Act of that year the trustees of the new turnpike took over the responsibility and paid the Corporation 5 guineas. Until the 18th century the bailiffs collected the tolls within the town, and eventually appointed tollers, and the accounts for 1510 and 1511 show that the market ward brought in more than the bridge ward. From about 1743 the practice began of farming the cart tolls at about £230 a year.

The Common Day Books record the appointment of various farmers and in some cases their bankruptcy. The advance both of trade and of *laissez-faire* doctrines led to a growing resentment at these payments and in 1786 the farmer for the time being lost a lawsuit brought by a carter who had refused to pay the toll, the court finding the Corporation had lost its prescriptive right to such tolls by the forfeiture of the town charters in 1381. A retrial was ordered but never took place, and the Corporation continued to lease the tolls at ever higher rates. By 1822 the tolls were bringing in £750 a year. Once again there was concerted resistance and three lawsuits followed, leading to the final judgement in 1829 depriving the Corporation of its right to levy the tolls. Over £4,000 had been spent on legal expenses and the Corporation was still in debt in 1833.

The right to take stallage or market tolls, however, remained. We hear of 8*d*. a year being paid for a stall in the 13th century, of 1*d*. a week before 1815 and a 1*d*. a day thereafter.

The profits of the mills also contributed to the fee farm. Whatever was the fate of the three mills controlled by Picot the sheriff, only one mill seems to have been farmed by the town under John's charter: the King's mill, which stood by the Bishop's mill at the end of Mill Lane and is shown on all maps of Cambridge down to its demolition in 1927. The Cambridge mill was profitable. In 1086 it brought in £9, and in 1157 the king granted an annuity of £3 to Solomon the goldsmith as a charge on the profits of the King's mill. Another charge was payable first to the Dunning family and later to Merton College. The accounts of the bailiffs in 1510 show that much of the dues was paid in kind. The Mayor and bailiff had full responsibility for upkeep and spent considerable sums on repairs, handing over the fixtures each year to their successors for an agreed sum. As has been seen, one of the four bailiffs was bailiff of the mill.

At various periods the town had temporary control of the two other mills, the mill of the Bishop of Ely and Newnham mill, which at the time of Domesday had been in the hands of Count Alan and had passed by way of the Zouches, Dunnings, and Mortimers to Gonville Hall by the end of the 15th century. In 1507, for instance, the town took a lease on the Bishop's mill for 99 years, and soon after they leased the Newnham mill from Gonville Hall. In 1518, however, both mills were being farmed at a substantial profit by private farmers. In 1566 the King's and Bishop's mills were leased jointly to one lessor.

Thenceforth they were under one roof, though the town never acquired the ownership of the Bishop's mill; though retaining its ancient name, it had become Crown property under Elizabeth I. In 1635 all three mills were farmed by one man, as on several later occasions. This represented a sound investment on the part of the town, as long as the mills continued to work. It constituted, however, an undesirable monopoly in the eyes of the University, who protested in 1601 that 'our neighbours of the town have all the mills here at their own command'.

The third item of the ancient Crown revenue is the profits of the town courts, to which were added after 1385 forfeitures and fines incurred by Cambridge men in the King's courts. The profits of the town courts diminished as their business dwindled, and they do not amount to very much in the Mayor's and bailiffs' accounts of 1510, but there are profits arising from the sales of waifs and strays.

When we turn to the treasurers' accounts, the items of expenditure become far more interesting. If the Mayor and bailiffs had a balance in hand they were expected, as Maitland conjectured, to spend it on a dinner. The treasurers, however, doubtless by town orders, were able to spend large sums of money on gifts to great men and to strolling players, on the wages of their Members of Parliament, on expenses of their officers going to London, on fees and salaries, on repairs to town property, on furbishing the town armaments and, of course, on dinners. What were the resources from which these funds were derived?

From the accounts of the Mayor and bailiffs and the treasurer's rolls we find that fines for offices, payments for taking up freedoms, and profits of the fairs figure in both sets of rolls. But whereas the profits of Reach and Midsummer fairs are slight, the steadily increasing profits of Sturbridge Fair, the payments for booths there and the proceeds of the Piepowder Court held there constitute a substantial and growing item in the treasurer's account. With the waning importance of the fair in the 18th century, the value of these items declined, but, at the same time, another source of revenue was rapidly appreciating: the real property rights of the Corporation as lords of the soil.

In the reign of Henry II, when the town first tried to acquire the *firma burgi*, it was still paying various small rents for different properties in the town and, as Maitland shows, as late as 1294 a Cambridge burgess is described as holding in chief of the king the tenement for which he pays hawgavel to the town. The Crown retained the right both to escheats and to the leasing of vacant sites all through the 13th century. In 1230, for instance, Nicholas Pilate offered 5 marks at the

Exchequer 'on behalf of the burgesses of Cambridge', for a certain void place in Cambridge for the use of the Franciscans, whilst in 1267, the Mayor and bailiffs had to pay rent for a messuage of the Earl of Leicester which had escheated to the Crown. The lawsuit of 1275 between Eleanor, the Queen mother, and the Bishop of Ely over the patronage of St. John's Hospital suggests another conclusion. The queen's counsel claimed that she, as tenant in dower of the town of Cambridge, had the presentation 'per burgenses qui tenuerunt predictam villam de domino rege ad feodifermam' and the jury found that the site of the hospital was a very poor, empty place belonging to the community of the town of Cambridge and that Henry Eldcorn had built upon it, *by the assent of the community*. The queen dowager claimed through the community, and the rights of the Crown to the vacant sites were exercised by the burgesses.

When in 1330 the town petitioned for leave to approve the lanes and waste places of the town, it seems probable that they were merely asking for the legalization of existing practice and that their plea was granted, though no answer is recorded. By 1347 the town was already drawing a substantial income from the leases of town property; the rents amounted to over £17. An inquest of 1353 expressly found that the brethren of the guild of Corpus Christi held the tenements which they wished to give to Corpus Christi College of the men of the town of Cambridge who held the town from the king. The Borough had become the mesne landlord. The rental of 1500 speaks not merely of shops, but of waste grounds, enclosed lanes, and footbridges whose tenants hold 'land and soil belonging to the town of Cambridge'.

The report of the Borough rate committee drawn up by Cooper in 1850 gives numerous instances of the founders of the colleges buying waste land from the town in addition to the house plots they purchase from individual burgesses. It is possible that Henry III had bought land from the men of Cambridge. It is certain that Henry VI bought a lane from the town for the site of King's College as Edward IV did for Queens' College.

The value of the properties rented by the town rose from about £17 in 1347 to over £22 in 1424, £70 in 1519 to £165 in 1570. After that it rose more gradually by £226 in 1680 to £247 in 1753. Then again it rose suddenly to £428 in 1805 and had reached £542 by 1832, according to the senior treasurer's evidence to the commissioners in 1833. The profits of the tolls were then £178; those of the fair had shrunk to £44. Rents brought in £542 14s. 6½d. and fines on leases £172.

The long series of leases of town property preserved in the town archives begins with a lease for 50 years from September 1500. The lessors are described as the Mayor, bailiffs, treasurers, and burgesses of the town. The lessee, John Serle, burgess, is granted a garden on the east side of Fair Yard Lane at a yearly rent of 2s. Hereon he was to build a house and keep it in repair. The Book of Orders of 1609 lays it down that every lease must contain a proviso not to alienate. An early instance of a long lease was one to Pembroke College in 1620 for 500 years at 1*s*. a year. Two years after this it was ordered that no lease was to be for more than 21 years except of waste lands, and in 1625 that all leases should be publicly registered. The growth of population in the early 17th century which led to subdivision of tenements and complaints by the University that the burgesses 'under color of being lords of the soil' were 'pestering every lane and corner of the town with unwholesome and base cottages', made the potential value of the town property more obvious. A regulation in 1677 that leases of town property should be granted only to free burgesses, to colleges or to parishes, paved the way for the jobbery of the 18th century.

Newton's Diary in 1669 mentions the appointment of a committee to view two houses that were to be granted by lease. The appointment of 'references' to report on applications for leases or their renewal became the routine procedure. In 1759 it was laid down that the Town Clerk should advertise in the newly-founded *Cambridge Journal* when a lease was out so that it might go to the highest bidder, and this was still the rule in 1777.

It seems probable, however, that the members of the Corporation were assisting each other to good bargains even before 1788, when the Mortlock régime was fully established. In 1786 it was provided that the Mayor should be on all references and in 1787 that he should nominate all references, and a by-law of 1791 repealed all previous by-laws about the leasing of town property and left the Mayor completely free to grant leases to persons who were not known to the Corporation. It was taken for granted, however, that members of the Corporation got better terms, and in 1833 a witness who had served on many references considered a 10 per cent. advantage as only reasonable.

The facts and figures in the lease-book and the evidence given in 1833 reveal reckless squandering of the town property at a moment when its value was fast appreciating. An information laid in Chancery by the anti-Mortlock faction in June 1788, charges the defendants with granting long leases of corporation estates at small rents. In 1789 leases began to be granted for 999 years as a regular practice and 30 such leases were granted between 1789 and 1800, for fines ranging from 5s. to £50 and for rents ranging from 1 to 10 guineas a year. 'All had good bargains but Alderman Butcher the best of all.'

Alderman Butcher, solicitor to Mortlock, and agent for the Duke and Duchess of Rutland, secured a lease of the whole of both sides of what is now Regent Street for £30, a frontage of 1,386 ft. which was worth 24s. a foot in 1810. He said at the time that he was so convinced that Cambridge was prospering that he would have the land at any price, and a well-known land speculator, not of the Corporation, would have paid anything for it. Butcher also acquired for 2 guineas a frontage of 345 feet at Maids' Causeway which he sold soon after for £345.

These bargains were the 'signal for a general scramble... amongst the corporators', and thus the Corporation shared out the potential land values of a town that was growing more rapidly than ever before in its history. In 1833 the commissioners learned of 62 leases for 999 years as well as 69 40-year leases. The remark of Common Councillor Starmer is notorious: 'he thought that the property belonged *bona fide* to the Corporation and they had a right to do what they liked with their own.' And indeed some £1,197 derived from the sale of property was entirely unaccounted for.

Besides the profits arising from lands rented or leased, there were certain realizable values in the commons over which the town exercised a landlord's control. The lands granted to Barnwell before the first charter had given the prior independent rights that were to cause recurrent trouble. But the responsibility of the town for the common grazing lands was exemplified in regulations by town ordinance from 1338 onwards, when an ordinance provided that every man who had cattle on the common pastures should herd them under the charge of the town herdsman. In 1275 and again in 1381 the right of the townsmen to drive their beasts from Greencroft to Estenhale across the Barnwell lands was asserted as the right of all the townsmen. In 1502 when a number of burgesses were presented in the court leet for putting out more than their fair share of beasts on the common, the Prior of Barnwell was one of the offenders, and four years later it was expressly stated that he is to be 'stinted' along with all the other inter-commoners.

But whether the Prior of Barnwell or the masters and scholars of the University or the burgesses were concerned, the common rights seem to have been appendant to holding of arable and the burgesses claimed full control over the 'stinting' of the commons and were prepared to inclose them on their own responsibility. They reserved to freemen the profitable right of planting willows on the banks of the ditches with which the marshier pastures were drained. The rising of 1549 was an apparently successful assertion of the rights of the inhabitants who were not freemen of the Borough and who held no ploughlands to a share in the use of the town commons. The regulations of 1551, 1583, and 1624 definitely recognized the rights of the inhabitants who were not members of the town oligarchy to which only substantial townsmen were admitted.

After 1624 peace descended on the commons of Cambridge, and when the arable fields were inclosed in 1802 and 1807 no particular interest seems to have been excited among the inhabitants who were not freemen. But in 1833 when the commissioners inquired about the Cambridge commons there was evidence that here also the Corporation was widely regarded as having failed to discharge its responsibilities. The dyking and planting of earlier years had been completely neglected, and the commons had deteriorated until they were a danger to health. On Sturbridge Common at fair time horses stood up to their knees in mud. The sum of £150 had been raised by subscription for the draining of one common.

To this the Corporation had contributed 10 guineas. Before draining it had not been worth more than 2*s*. 6*d*. an acre; after draining, it could be let for £10 an acre. The Cambridge commons, which in 1833 were 'of very little benefit' either to the town or to the Corporation, escaped inclosure in 1841 and 1850, and are now available for grazing, to the extent of 226 acres, from Old May Day to Old Candlemas Day.

David Mills

Economic History

Medieval Trade and Industry, p. 86. Fairs, p. 91. Jews, p. 95. Banks, p. 96. Modern Economic Development, p. 97.

Medieval Trade and Industry

The economic importance of Cambridge turned on its position as a centre of communications. It was and is a marketing centre for the shire and it served as the clearing house for the agricultural produce of the surrounding countryside whilst its accessibility from so many directions made it the most natural centre for the most famous fair in England.

First in importance came the river-borne trade. From 1118 to 1845, when the opening of the railway to London dealt the river trade its death-blow, the waterway from Cambridge to the Wash was one of the main thoroughfares of trade in the Eastern Midlands. In the 12th century, the river traffic went by the old Well Stream by Outwell and Wisbech and the Nene, but before the middle of the 13th century this outlet was silting up and the Ouse had been diverted to flow, more directly, by Wiggenhall to Lynn. It was Lynn that was the port of Cambridge down to the 19th century.

In 1620 the public orator called the Cam 'our river . . . by means of which we enjoy the wealth of the neighbouring country', and the passionate opposition of both town and gown to the draining of the Bedford level from 1607 to 1653 was due to the fear that, as Fuller put it, 'the river Grant or Cam running by Cambridge will have its stream dried up by the draining of the fens'. Fuller himself admitted, however, 'It seems that Cambridge was then more frighted than since it hath been hurt, now the project is effected'.

Nevertheless, apprehension continued; Denver Sluice, it was feared, would obstruct the 'free and easy passage' of the vessels bringing coals, fish, salt, and foreign merchandise from Lynn to Cambridge, and petitioners still besieged Parliament from 1670 to 1745. In 1702 a bill for making the Cam, or Grant, more navigable was introduced on the joint instance of town and gown, and in 1703 the Conservators of the Cam were established by Act of Parliament. Three conservators were to be appointed by the University, three by the Mayor and aldermen, and five by the county magistrates at Quarter Sessions. Together they were empowered to improve the navigation from the Queen's mill to Clayhithe, and to make orders, levy tolls for upkeep, borrow money, hold up boats, and take distresses.

With their powers revised by legislation, the conservators still function, though with lessened importance. The proposal to link the navigation of the Cam with the Thames by canal was first made in 1665, and renewed persistently from 1782 onwards. In spite of the opposition of the conservators an Act authorizing a canal from Stortford to Clayhithe was passed in 1812, but the canal was never made. The high days of inland navigation were over, although as late as the 1860's we hear of the 'half a hundred black barges' that went downstream to Lynn and came upstream to Cambridge 'laden with coal or heaped high with turf and sedge'.

Of the goods for which Cambridge was a clearing-house, corn was the most important. On the estates of Ely Abbey, as we hear in the early 13th century, the villeins carried the abbot's corn to be sold at Cambridge from Hadstock, Great Shelford, Little Gransden, Willingham, Doddington, Streatham, Wilburton, and Fen Ditton, whilst on the Ramsey manors, the villeins owed carrying services from February to August, as long as the surplus grain held out, either to Cambridge or to London. These are merely two instances indicating the importance of Cambridge as a centre of the corn trade. The sixteen burgesses who were fined for exporting corn by water without royal licence in 1177 were some of them wealthy enough to be liable in 10 marks. Corn to the value of £67 12s. was shipped to Norway from Cambridge by John's orders in 1202.

Cambridge was again forbidden to export corn because of scarcity in 1351 and under Elizabeth I a protest that the local shortage was sending up the price of grain in Cambridge market 'to the pinching of poor scholars' bellies' evoked from the Privy Council the reply that the shire of Cambridge had been accustomed to convey its grain by water to Lynn and thence to London for the victualling of that city and that it was very necessary both for the help of the city and for encouragement to the husbandmen that the traffic should continue. The Council was only prepared to prohibit export if the corn was being sent overseas and not to London. As the corn merchants could get 10½d. to 6s. a quarter more in London than in Cambridge and transport by water was easy, it is not surprising that corn went 'in a continuous stream' to feed other districts. The *Liber Albus* of London shows that corn went by land also, by way of Ware, and malt also went to London from Cambridge from the 14th century on.

There was also a considerable trade in fish by the river. Sea-fish came up from Lynn as corn went down, and in the 16th century the coal trade began. In 1544 the Corporation indemnified the Mayor, with others, who had ventured to Newcastle-upon-Tyne for four shiploads of coal. Again in 1702 the Mayor, bailiffs, and burgesses of Cambridge petitioned the Lord High Admiral for armed protection of the ships that imported sea-coal, salt, and other merchandise for the needs of the town and University of Cambridge from Newcastle and other foreign parts. As late as 1804 Cambridge was said to be the head of the inland navigation from Lynn whereby it had an extensive trade in coal and corn, and as the 17th-century drainage of the fens brought about what Fuller called 'a deluge and inundation of plenty', their manifold produce came on to Cambridge, with imports from more distant regions. *The Foreigners' Companion* describes the situation in 1748:

The purest wine they receive by the Way of Lynn: Flesh, Fish, Wild-Fowl, Poultry, Butter, Cheese, and all Manner of Provisions, from the adjacent Country: Living is cheap: Coals from seven-pence to nine-pence a Bushel; Turf, or rather Peat, four shillings a thousand; Sedge, with which the Bakers heat their Ovens, four shillings per hundred sheaves: These, together with Osiers, Reeds, and Rushes used in several Trades, are daily imported by the River Cam. Great quantities of Oil, made of Flax-seed, Cole-seed, Hemp and other Seeds, ground or press'd by the numerous Mills in the Isle of Ely, are brought up by this River also: and the Cakes, after the Oil is press'd out, afford the Farmer an excellent Manure to improve his Grounds. By the River they also receive 1500 or 2000 Firkins of Butter every week, which is sent by waggon to London. Besides which, great quantities are made in the neighbouring villages, for the use of the University and Town and brought in new every Morning almost. Every Pound of this Butter is roll'd, and drawn out to a Yard in Length, about the Bigness of a Walking-cane; which is mentioned as peculiar to this Place.

That flax itself came long before to Cambridge is suggested by the occurrence under Edward I of the name Flaxhythe as one of a succession of wharves that ran along the river bank from the common hythe just north of the Great Bridge. These were 'Dame Nichole's Hythe', 'Cornhythe', 'Flaxhythe', 'Salthythe', and 'Cholleshithe' just below the Small Bridges.

The close commercial relations with Lynn produced a good deal of friction. In 1286 the Commonalty of Lynn vindicated its exemption from payment of toll and stallage at Cambridge. In 1535 Cambridge was claiming exemption from toll if its ships discharged their merchandise at Lynn. The grant of two fairs to Lynn was revoked in 1541 lest Sturbridge Fair should suffer. In 1551 outstanding disputes between the two towns were submitted to arbitration and a carefully drafted award secured to the burgesses of Lynn rights of purchase to a part of the Cambridge cargoes and defined the payments owed by Cambridge burgesses for tying up their ships in the harbour, as a contribution towards the upkeep of the haven, the beacons, and the buoys. The burgesses of Lynn in return were secured dockage rights at Cambridge at the time of Sturbridge Fair. Further disputes, however, recurred towards the end of Elizabeth I's reign and another award was given in 1599 by two arbitrators, one being Attorney-General Coke.

Duties on salt, corn, and sea coal had been exacted by the burgesses of Lynn, cargoes had been seized, and Lynn porters had refused to work for burgesses of Cambridge. A Lynn cargo of pitch and tar had been confiscated at Sturbridge Fair for failure to pay ground dues. Once again, the exemption of Lynn burgesses from toll was upheld but the groundage fees were to be paid.

Cambridge was and is an important market centre. The market stands on one of the oldest inhabited sites of the Borough and perpetually reminds the observer that the town is older than the University and has an independent *raison d'être*. No grant of a market by charter was necessary; it was established by local need and ancient custom well before the Norman Conquest. The regulations in the *Cross Book* make frequent reference to the buying and selling not only of corn and butter but of poultry, milk, garden produce, and meat. Among the earliest ordinances preserved are those forbidding the setting up of butchers', fishers', or tanners' stalls in the market except on market day.

An ordinance of 1377 lays down the location of the various stalls or tables in the market and forbids the sale of bad meat. Each burgess was entitled to one free stall but no more. An ordinance of 12 February 1579 provided that 'all the fresh-water fish and sea fish brought to the town and all the common fishmongers which usually have stood in the market over against the new shambles shall from henceforth be sold on the Pease Market Hill and have and keep their standing there'. The new fish market, supplied with paving and penthouses by the help of a contribution from Dr. Hatcher, was still kept until 1949 where it was placed in 1579.

The shambles where the meat was exposed for sale were on the south side of the market in front of the Guildhall. The corn market where poultry and butter also were sold was to the north. The garden market was in the middle, to the east of the market cross; the fruit, flower, and vegetable stalls which make Cambridge one of the best markets for garden produce in England occupy the same position today but have spread further afield. The milk market was west of the market cross. Petty Cury, mentioned as *parva cokeria* in 1330, took its name from the cookshops which supplied the needs of those coming in from the country; it is possible that the eastern side of the market square was once the Great Cury or Cook's Row.

The old street names of Cambridge are evidence of the trades plied in the town. Butchery Row and Slaughterhouse Lane led to Hog Hill where hogs and horses were sold. Cordwainer Row, 1322 and the leather market, 1362, with Tanners' Hall indicate the presence of the leather-workers. Other lanes and rows mostly unidentified but probably in the modern market square give further indications. Shearer's Row, 1512, Felters Street, Comber's Lane, 1319, and the Duddery, 1561, are evidence of workers in wool, while Broiderers'

Lane, 1561, like Goldsmith's Row, 1589, testifies to more elaborate craftsmanship. The Cutlers' Row, 1297, is matched by the Sheathers' Lane, 1508, and the Smiths', 1271, by the Braziers', 1589. The Lorimers' Row, 1299, housed the makers of metal harness fittings, and Smearmongers' Row, 1330, the sellers of tallow. Potters' Row, 1249, furnished table ware, supplied with comestibles not only from the corn market and milk market, but from Butter Row, Cheese Market, and Malt Market, and the Poultry Row, 1388. With the Apothecaries' Row, 1286, we reach more sophisticated trades.

Other evidence of the trades plied in Cambridge comes from the callings of the various burgesses who witness deeds or serve as town officials. The cartulary of St. John's Hospital supplies the names of tailors, girdlers, cobblers, tanners, bakers, skinners, cheesemongers, and a writer and an illuminator to which the St. Radegund's deeds add another illuminator in 1274, and a parchment-maker. Among the various trades practised by Cambridge mayors are those of litster, skinner, grocer, goldsmith, waxchandler, baker, brewer, butcher, draper, confectioner, fishmonger, haberdasher, vintner.

Early evidence of a woollen industry in Cambridge is provided by the presentment of four drapers in 1261 and six in 1286 for selling cloth against the assize. The cloth may have been imported then, and the first webster mentioned, in 1440, was an alien, but in 1449–51 cloth was woven for the nuns of St. Radegund's by a Cherry Hinton man, and fulled and shorn, it seems, in Cambridge. Fullers and shearers are mentioned, as well as a silkwoman, in 1491 and 1512. Tenter yards on the lower slopes of the castle grounds are referred to in the 17th century, and Hobson's Spinning House employed many hands until 1800. Textile workers are mentioned again in 1719, when in a petition to Parliament the Corporation together with the woollen drapers, mercers, sergemakers, say-makers, websters, and wool-combers inhabiting the town complained of unemployment caused in the woollen manufacture in and about Cambridge by the general use of Indian calicoes and linens.

The drapery business of the second John Mortlock founded the fortunes of his son, and in 1791 the woolcombers are mentioned again as celebrating St. Blaise's day with a procession. The sellers of wine who were also penalized in 1261 and 1286 may well have imported their wine from London since Stephen of Hauxton had a partner dwelling there. In 1510 there are details of a Cambridge vintner who supplied five colleges, a number of inns, and 40 private customers with malmsey, rumney, red claret, white claret, and bastard, and the trade, regulated and licensed by the University, became one of the most important in Cambridge.

The assessments for the subsidy of 1512, though extant only for Market and Preachers' Wards, give valuable information as to

Cambridge industries. Brewers, freemasons, tailors, and shoemakers preponderate, and there are suggestions that the leather-working trades have been stimulated by alien immigrants. Nicholas Williamson, 'Dutchman' and alien born, employing eight servants and apprentices, was a shoemaker, as was the 'Dutchman', John Petyrson. In 1440, of the 23 alien householders reported in Cambridge, seven were cordwainers, one of them employing six other Dutchmen in his business. The aliens had come from Brabant, Holland and Zealand, as well as Scotland, Ireland, France, and Germany. Other trades reported in 1512 were those of thatcher, tiler, cooper, carpenter, staffmaker, raffman, and paviour, in addition to others already noted.

John Lete, smith, employed ten servants and apprentices, and William Barbour, goldsmith, had six; on the other hand a large number of 'common labourers', paying the lowest rate of taxation, were to be found in Preachers' Ward, balancing the wealthier inhabitants of Market Ward. The paper-mill on the Newmarket road, first mentioned in 1557, was probably older. The development of the printing and bookbinding trades from 1521 under University protection has been described elsewhere; it was to become a permanent activity, unlike the manufacture of saltpetre, frequently mentioned in the early 17th century.

As we have seen, the guild merchant of Cambridge early lost any economic significance it may have had. Cunningham, noting mention of wool-combers and skinners, failed to trace any craft guild in connexion with the clothing trade. There seems to be documentary evidence of only one craft guild in Cambridge. On 5 May 1590 the Corporation ordained that every cordwainer, shoemaker, or cobbler, who should set up shop in Cambridge and therein exercised his trade, must not only have served his apprenticeship but must be licensed by the masters and wardens of the Cordwainers' Company, presumably of London. The cordwainers in the town were to meet every year to elect a master and two wardens with power to search all the wares produced by the trade in Cambridge.

The fact that nothing more is known of this craft guild and that no similar ordinance exists for any other craft may possibly be due to the fact that no Common Day Book survives for the period 1582 to 1610. We owe the copy of this ordinance to Metcalfe. It is unfortunate that for 30 years of crowded and prosperous Borough history our most valuable source should be lacking.

Fairs

Three of the four Cambridge fairs are of purely local interest. Reach Fair, held at Rogationtide, appears to have been already in existence in 1201. If so it may be associated with Henry I's grant of the monopoly of river-borne trade. In 1279, however, the Cambridge jurors described the Rogationtide fair as held 'in the town of Cambridge' and the jurors of Stone Hundred referred to 'a certain fair' as being shared equally between the king and the Prior of Ely. In 1388 an inquest in Cambridge found that the Prior of Ely held one-third of the fair and the burgesses two-thirds. However that may be, as far back as the evidence goes, the fair was held at Reach some 10 miles from Cambridge and proclaimed by the Mayor of Cambridge.

The roll of the Pie Powder Court survives for 1508 and shows that there were dealings there in corn, in cloth, in shoes, and in horses, but the profits in 1511 were only 6s. 2d. Newton gives a brief account of the visit of the Mayor and aldermen to Reach in 1669; but the proclamation in state had become a heavy cost to the Corporation by the 18th century. Its limits were defined in 1850 as extending to half a mile from the site of the ancient chapel. It is still opened annually by the Mayor on Rogation Monday with due formalities, though it is now merely an amusement fair with a small sale of horses and ponies.

By Newton's day, Midsummer Fair was also town property. It had been granted to the Canons of Barnwell by John in 1211, and by Henry's Charter of 1229 it was to last from the vigil of St. Etheldreda to the third day following 22–25 June. By 1279 St. Awdry had yielded to St. John and Midsummer Fair became its name, though Greencroft did not become Midsummer Green until 1501. The burgesses who had made good their claim to quittance from fair dues as early as 1232 and had adjusted other disputes in 1294, took a yearly lease of the fair in

1496 and acquired full right over it, in a general settlement of outstanding differences with the priory, in 1506. Newton describes the formal opening in 1669: the Mayor attended by the aldermen in their scarlet and the Four and Twenty in their gowns proclaimed the fair 'once against the Cock, and the other in the water fayre beyond the soap barrells neere the Iron and next the River banke'; the serjeant cryer proclaimed the court at the door of the booth; and the corporation dinner followed.

There seems to be no account of the commodities sold, though in 1290 we hear of a merchant selling knives, gloves, and girdles, but by the later 18th century the traffic in earthenware had become so important as to give it the name of Pot Fair. It had come to last for a fortnight, and to be a fashionable event, falling as it did at the time of Commencement. Gunning describes it 'in all its glory' in 1785, attended by gentry from the town and neighbourhood and the adjoining counties, with fellows of colleges, and masters of arts, four or five arm in arm making the most splendid assemblage, and raffles for pictures, china, and millinery taking place every evening at the booths. Twenty years later it was still held for a fortnight, and in 1833 it brought in a larger profit than Sturbridge Fair, but by 1840 it had declined, and by the Cambridge Corporation Act of 1850 it was limited to its original four days. Though it has no economic significance today it is annually proclaimed by the Mayor on 22 June.

Garlick Fair, granted to St. Radegund's by Stephen, was held on their own land at the junction of Jesus Lane and Park Street, formerly called Garlic Lane, from 14 to 16 August. It was never large. It went to Jesus College with the other endowments of St. Radegund and was still in existence in 1808, though 'nearly abolished'.

Sturbridge Fair, called in 1589 'by far the largest and most famous fair in all England', had very modest beginnings. Its phenomenal growth is the outstanding evidence of the geographical advantages of Cambridge as a centre for commerce. It was granted, again by John, to the Leper Hospital of St. Mary Magdalene, whose chapel still stands on the old fair ground, near where the Newmarket Road crosses a small tributary of the Granta by the bridge once called the Steers' bridge. By 1279 the hospital had ceased to have any patients, but the burgesses claimed to appoint its warden, and by 1376 had established their right to the profits of the fair. This right was attacked by Henry VIII in 1539 and the burgesses, faced by an information of *quo warranto*, offered 1,000 marks for a regrant of their 'usurped liberties', and apparently continued to exercise them. The charter of 1589, procured by the good offices of Lord North, declared the fair theirs from time immemorial though the University as clerk of the market could still oust the Mayor's judicial rights in the fair. More profitable than jurisdiction, probably, was the letting of booths and places in the fair ground. After 1403 every burgess was entitled to one booth free, but the treasurer's accounts for 1561–2 show £33 1s. 9d. received from rents of booths.

In 1279 the fair was held on 13 and 14 September. By 1516 it was lasting from 24 August to 29 September; the intervening stages are only hinted at. About 1349 the accounts of St. Mary des Prés show heavy expenditure at Sturbridge Fair on fish, horseshoes, mats, baskets, and cloth. Two years later the king's deputy alnager seized 38 cloths at the fair for infringement of the assize of cloth. In 1376 ordinances concerning booths at the fair began to appear in the Cross Book, while the date of the dedication feast of Holy Trinity Church was shifted to 9 October to avoid the multifold business of the parishioners about the fair. In 1419 the University and the Mayor of London laid claim to the custody of the assize of bread, wine, and ale at the fair. An ordinance of 1427, not cited by Cooper, shows that the traditional layout of the fair was already producing street names; the booths in the street called 'Chepe' raised every year in the 'Overfeyre' were not to be permanent structures.

About this time silken and goldembroidered goods, iron, and imported timber were sold at the fair. The sale of local fish was still very important, but the fair was beginning to be the mart for all manner of products brought from London and more distant workshops. In 1450–1 the nuns of St. Radegund's bought there, besides fish and timber, pepper, soap, and a churn. The proclamation of the fair in 1549 mentioned various ales and wines, bread, fish salt and fresh of all sorts, flax, yarn, woollen and linen cloth, silk, pitch, tar, coal, charcoal, faggots, salt, hay, and grain. By 1561 the layout of the fair included the Duddery, Birchin Lane, Chepesyde, Hadley Rowe and the Back Booths and Bury Booths, and in 1586 the temporarily erected tolbooth, counsel house and court house on the fair ground are mentioned. In 1583 there were booksellers at the fair, and in 1606 'a pair of claricalls' was bought there. The printing of '400 passes against Sturbridge Fayre' in the treasurer's accounts for 1616 indicates that the fair was becoming as densely thronged as when Bunyan described it in the *Pilgrim's Progress*.

Though prohibited on account of the plague in 1625, 1630, 1636, and 1637, the fair was held all through the Civil War, and it was at this time that it was described as 'the most plentiful of wares in all England, most fairs in other parts being but markets in comparison, being an Ambion, as well going on ground as swimming by water by the benefit of a navigable river'. An antidote to its sideshows, such as stage plays and dancing horses, was provided by the appointment of a 'preaching minister'.

An account of *A trip to Stirbitch Fair* in 1700 speaks of vast quantities of hops from the adjacent counties; of Garlick Row, where milliners, toymen, cabinet-makers, and perfumers are found; of Cork Row, where book auctions are held; of Cheapside, where wholesale linen drapers, silk men, ironmongers, leather-sellers, and tobacconists do business; of the Duddery, where Norwich stuffs and Yorkshire cloths are sold and packets of wool weighing at least a ton. It is this wholesale trade which figures most impressively in Defoe's famous account of the year 1723. He calls the fair the greatest in the world, surpassing those at Leipzig, Frankfort, and Nuremburg.

The wholesaler's pocket-book transactions, especially in heavy goods like iron, salt, groceries, wine, and wool exceeded those in goods actually there; he speaks of £10,000 deals. The two articles which he calls 'peculiars of the fair' are wool and hops 'there is scarce any price fix'd for Hops in England till they know how they sell at Sturbridge Fair'. The hops of Kent and Surrey, he explains, were shipped by water to the fair field and there purchased by brewers not only from the midland and eastern counties but also from the northern counties and Scotland. The wool came principally from Lincolnshire, where the longest staple is found; some £60,000 worth had been sold at one fair.

The manufactured cloths, woollens, and cottons from Yorkshire and Lancashire, the serges, druggets, shalloons, Cantaloons, Kersies, and DuRoys from Somerset and Devon, and the sackings, blankets, rugs, and other upholsterers' goods from Kidderminster filled up the booths of the Duddery, where as much as £109,000 worth of goods had been sold in one week. Hardware from Birmingham, knives from Sheffield, glassware and stockings from Nottingham and Leicester helped to draw the confluence of people from all parts of England.

Yet for Cambridge itself Sturbridge Fair was more of a social than an economic event. The fair was proclaimed in state by Mayor and Corporation, riding out in a procession whose Tudor pomp was kept up until 1790. The Vice-Chancellor and University officers celebrated its opening with a dinner at the Oyster House which still stands in Garlic Row. The town inns and hackney drivers and boatmen made their profit, but could not handle the crowds without extraneous help. Town and gown alike profited by the one chance in the year to see a stage play. The husbandmen who had stripped the cornfields by 24 August found them well manured with fair refuse when the booths were cleared away by 29 September. With the possible exception of the Horse-Fair, Cambridge had little more than a site to contribute to the greatest fair in Christendom.

The pocket-book transactions of the wholesale men noted by Defoe presaged the decline of the fair, the stages of which can be measured at intervals. In 1749 Carter describes it as lasting only from 7 to 28 September, 'though the greatest part is over in a fortnight'. In 1762 the coal, pottery, cheese, wool, and hop fairs were still thronged, and ironmongers, silversmiths, hatters, silk-mercers, toymen, shoemakers, oilmen, and others were said to do good business, whilst the horse fair on 25 September drew crowds of gentry and farmers. Sixteen London tradesmen were listed as attending the fair, and the Mayor still held the pie powder court, but it now began on 18 September and lasted only a fortnight, and the numbers had fallen greatly. Gunning speaks of it reminiscently as 'in all its glory' in 1789, but mainly in its festive aspect.

The state procession was abolished in 1790. In 1804, though considerable business in wool, hops, leather, cheese, and iron was still done, there were only 8 or 10 London coaches where once there had been 60 or more. The fair still lasted for a fortnight in 1830. By 1840, in place of the many streets of old, there was only one range of booths. In 1897 the fair lasted for three days only, and apart from 'Ossferdye' dealt with nothing but toys, confectionery, and amusements. Twenty years later only the horse fair survived. The fair was proclaimed for the last time in September 1933 to an audience of three. By Home Office order, confirming a resolution of the Town Council, it was abolished 5 July 1934.

Jews

In the 13th century the quarter called the Jewry was that between All Saints by the Hospital and the Round Church. The lane now known as All Saints' Passage is called the Jews' Street about 1219; a number of grants of that period to St. Radegund's are of land in All Saints parish, 'in' or 'next to the Jewry', and both St. Sepulchre and All Saints are described in 1279 as being in the Jewry. There is clear evidence also that Jews lived in the parishes both of St. Clement and of the Holy Sepulchre, and the Jew Bonenfaunt, hanged about 1275 for clipping coin, owned a void place in which King's Hall was later interested. Cole believed, on the other hand, that the Jews congregated chiefly in the area between Butcher Row and the old Guildhall. It is certain that they had a synagogue on the site of the Guildhall, by the house of Benjamin the Jew. Stokes, the leading authority on the subject, believes that the Jews moved from the neighbourhood of the Guildhall to that of All Saints: in any case, there is no reason to think that they were ever officially segregated; they lived side by side with Christians.

There were Jews in Cambridge by the time of Niel, Bishop of Ely, who pawned a silver cross to the Cambridge Jews presumably about 1140. From their contribution to the tax levied on all the Jews of England in 1159, it seems that the Cambridge Jewry ranked fifth amongst those of England, after London, Norwich, Lincoln, and Southampton. It was to two Cambridge financiers that Richard of Anesty applied for loans in the same year; one of them, Comitissa, had many such transactions, and her son continued in the business. In the mid-13th century the Jews were making an important contribution to estate development by advancing ready money to country gentlemen. The list of bonds in the Cambridge *Archa* for the years 1224–40 gives a very good notion of the extent to which burgesses and country gentry were drawing on

Jewish capital; Harvey fitz Eustace is among the debtors. This led to some resentment on the part of the lesser nobility and may account for the brutality with which the 'disinherited' barons from the Isle of Ely raided the Jewry of Cambridge, slew many of its inhabitants and carried off their valuables on 12 August 1266; ignoring the special command of Henry III in the previous April that none should molest the Jews and their property.

The Jews of Cambridge, like those of many other towns, sent representatives to an assembly in 1241 which agreed to pay the king 20,000 marks, but three years later another tax of 60,000 was imposed before the first one was paid off. The contribution of Cambridge was over £110. The records of the Exchequer of Jews show that over 60 Cambridge Jews were lending money to Christians in the period 1234 to 1270, and Jews from Cambridge are found taking part in financial transactions in at least five other towns. They constituted undoubtedly a very important element in the economic life of the Borough. But their business activities were cut short abruptly by the grant to Eleanor, the Queen Mother, in January 1275, that no Jew should dwell in a town which she held in dower. As a result Jews were expelled from Cambridge, as from Gloucester, Marlborough, and Worcester, fifteen years before their general exodus in 1290. The chest of debts was transferred to Huntingdon and, when the inquisitors visited Cambridge in 1279, their houses had apparently escheated to the queen and had in many instances been purchased by burgesses. Only some twenty houses are enumerated as having belonged to Jews.

As moneylenders the Jews were replaced by the goldsmiths, such as William Barbour, wealthiest of the Cambridge residents rated for the subsidy in 1512, or Nicholas Symond, one of the alien immigrants, who became a freeman of Cambridge in 1521 and town treasurer in 1531.

Banks

The first bank in Cambridge was that opened in 1780 by John Mortlock. Its beginnings are thus described by Gunning.

At the death of his father, Mr. Mortlock came into possession of a profitable business, a large sum in ready money, and considerable landed property. . . . To the business left him by his father he added that of a banker, which engaged him in a variety of transactions for which at that time it was difficult to find an agent. He received dividends, purchased stock, and furnished letters of credit to such members of the county, town and university who were desirous of not running the risk of losing their guineas on their way to London by an encounter with highwaymen and pickpockets. These accommodations, liberally and cheerfully granted to all applicants without distinction of party, made him very popular. The circulation of his notes was for some time very confined, for even notes of the Bank of England were at that period received with distrust by the gentry of the county and positively refused by farmers.

Not only in 1833 but from the first the importance of the bank as the basis of Mortlock's political influence was recognized, and the run upon it by University and county clients in May 1784 was a deliberate reply to Mortlock's success in securing the receivership of the county for his banking partner, Francis. But Mortlock's credit stood, and in February 1785 he was able to tell the Duke of Rutland that he had discharged every engagement of his banking house and had real property clear to the amount of £33,000. The bank was at first housed in the premises of the draper's shop he had inherited from his father, at the corner of Rose Crescent. The drawers in which the cloth had been stored were used until the bank was transferred, probably about 1786, to the new bank house on the site of the old gateway of the Austin Friars in Bene't Street, purchased by Mortlock in 1783. Here the business was carried on by Mortlock, in due course banker to both University and Borough, and after his death by his third son Thomas, who was assisted by his nephews, Charles and Edmund. On Thomas's death the bank passed to Edmund, who ran it in partnership with Gilbert Ainsty from 1866 to 1888. In 1889 it was registered as a limited company and in 1896 was amalgamated with Barclay & Co. In 1955 its business was still conducted in the premises built by Mortlock.

Mortlock's eldest son, John, had been his assistant but quarrelled with him, and left to join forces, from 1817 to 1819, with Skrine and Barker's in Trinity Street. From the resolution of a public meeting in 1797 to accept the notes of Cambridge banks in all payments, it would appear that Mortlock had rivals before the end of the century, though according to Gunning he took the compliments to himself. But the second bank on record is Foster's, opened 11 November 1813, at 55 Bridge Street, opposite Jordan's Yard. In 1820 besides Foster's and Mortlock's in Sidney Street, there were Skrine and Barker's, later Barker's, in Trinity Street, and Hollick & Co. on Market Hill. Humphrey's Bank in Trumpington Street appeared in 1825, and Hollick's closed soon after. Fisher's Bank in Petty Cury is mentioned in 1837. Barker's Bank failed in 1841. About 1846 Humphrey's merged in the London and County Bank which in 1911 was in turn absorbed by the Westminster Bank. Foster's Bank, originally associated with Mortlock's, moved in 1836 to 14 Trinity Street, once the property of Mortlock's protégé, Forlow, and occupied in 1955 by Matthew's Café. In 1898 it moved to 3 Sidney Street, where in 1905 it was amalgamated with the Capital and Counties Bank, to be absorbed in 1919 into Lloyds Bank. The old name, Foster's Bank, is still cut on the stonework, as Mortlock's name appears on Barclay's cheques. Of the other members of the Big Five, the National Provincial established a branch at 6 King's Parade in 1909, and the Midland at 18 Petty Cury in

1914. Martin's Bank appeared at 30 Market Hill in 1939. The District Bank has recently opened a branch at 9 Trinity Street.

Modern Economic Development

To judge from the estimates of 6,490 in 1587 and 7,778 for 1728 the population of Cambridge had increased but slowly before the 19th century. From 1801 exact figures are available. Between that year and 1951 the population of the Borough increased from 10,087 to an estimated 91,170, and its area from 3,233 to 10,061 acres, 2,224 having been added in 1912 and 4,603 in 1935. The spectacular increase in the parish of St. Andrew the Less from 252 in 1801 to 11,776 in 1851 can be paralleled by the all-over increase of 20,000 between 1931 and 1951. Of these only 3,380 persons were added by the territorial extension of 1935. These figures represent an economic transformation.

The causes contributing to the accelerated expansion of the early 19th century were, in part, common to all England the increased expectation of life resulting from advances in hygiene and the stimulus to agriculture caused by the French Wars, which particularly affected an important market-town. The Inclosure Acts of 1801 and 1807 relieved the congestion in the centre of the town and rendered possible the rapid extension of the builtup area over the old open fields. The great increase in the number of undergraduates between

1810 and 1820 must have also led to increased trade and employment.

The opening of the railway in 1845, though it ultimately killed the river trade, added a new occupation and, it might be said, a new quarter to Cambridge in Romsey Town. By bringing Cambridge into closer touch with the London market it stimulated the development of industries. Brick and tile works at Cherry Hinton and Coldham's Lane, cement works at Romsey Town, flour-milling, sausage-making, brewing, and malting, occupied increasing numbers, as did building and construction work and the old-established industry of printing, which in 1901 occupied 286 men in the town.

Up to the outbreak of the First World War it would be true to say that the main cause of this industrial expansion was the development of the University, whose numbers increased threefold between 1861 and 1921 with the resulting stimulus to all the occupations concerned with supplying its needs, not only building and printing, but retail and victualling trades and personal service. Even in 1898 it was not true to say 'if the University did not exist there would be but little reason for the existence of the Town'. By 1950 only about 6 per cent. of the working population of the Cambridge district were employed by the University and colleges.

To this change several causes have contributed; the continued growth in importance of the town as a market and shopping centre, which has been helped by the development of motor transport; the establishing of Cambridge as the headquarters of East Anglian regional administration, and the development of the industries connected with applied sciences, mostly originated for and by University agencies, but now of national importance. The early history of the Cambridge Instrument Company, which had its beginnings in 1881 and was first formally registered in 1895, has already been told. Its principal products in 1950 can be classified as temperature-measuring instruments, engineering instruments, electrical instruments, chemical engineering instruments, physical instruments, such as seismographs, and physiological and medical instruments, such as the electro-cardiograph. Its development of the required apparatus forwarded the rapid expansion of the study of atomic physics.

An undertaking on an even larger scale also began by supplying the needs of the University. W. G. Pye had worked in the Cavendish Laboratory before he started his own business in Cambridge in 1896; it was after 1918 that his firm began to specialize in wireless. The Pye Radio Company, Ltd. was formed in 1929, and since then expansion has been rapid. During the Second World War work was concentrated on radar and radio-telegraphy for the services, and gun-sights, radio-activated fuses, and airnavigation equipment were also manufactured. Since 1945 television has taken the first place.

Pye Radio has devised apparatus for the B.B.C. and was in 1952 the largest manufacturer of television sets in Great Britain. Pye Telecommunications supplies short-wave sets for the use of the military and the police, as well as for ambulances and taxis. Pye Radio was the pioneer in Europe of colour television, and its equipment is used for televising operations in London medical schools and for deep-sea underwater work. It has branch firms in Eire, Northern Ireland, Canada, South Africa, Australia, and New Zealand, and its installations are used in the U.S.A. In 1950 the Pye group of companies operating in Cambridge included, besides Pye Radio, Unicam Industries, Ltd., Labgear, Ltd., Cathodeon, Ltd., Pye Telecommunications, and Pye Industrial Electronics.

Besides other branches of electrical engineering, Cambridge industries in 1950 included the manufacture of agricultural implements, rope-making, brush-making, gun-making, boat-building, motor-body building, cement manufacture, and the manufacture both of hard asphalte and of bituminous mastic asphalte for covering roofs and lining buildings below ground level.

The early history of the printing trade in Cambridge has been told elsewhere. Apart from the University Press, which employs some 300 men, printing has in Cambridge been associated with the local newspaper offices. The first Cambridge newspaper, the *Cambridge Journal and the Weekly Flying Post*, appeared on 22 September 1744.

It was started by Robert Walker and Thomas James and printed 'next the Theatre Coffee House'. By 1764 the *Cambridge Journal* was selling in London, Stamford, Ely, St. Ives, Huntingdon, Boston, and Spalding, and drawing advertisements from Northampton, Lincoln, and Lynn. Its sympathies were Tory, but its account of elections, even that of 1754, were impartial. It ran a serial novel in 1749. It was, however, losing ground well before the appearance of its rival, the *Cambridge Chronicle*, on 30 October 1762, published at the same price of 2½d. weekly, and definitely aimed at a University public. In September 1766 the *Journal* was absorbed by the *Chronicle* which, though it devoted little space as a rule to Cambridge news, is a valuable source for municipal politics and contains advertisements of corporation posts. Its advancing Toryism, however, left scope for a more liberal paper and on 20 July 1793 the *Cambridge Intelligencer* was launched by Benjamin Flower.

It was almost the only provincial newspaper in the kingdom to denounce the French War as 'absurd and wicked' and in 1799 its editor was found guilty of breach of privilege of the House of Lords for an attack upon the Bishop of Llandaff and punished by six months' imprisonment and a fine of £100. He left Cambridge some five years later and his paper came to an end in June 1803. The flag of opposition was raised again when Weston Hatfield issued the first number of the *Cambridge and Hertford Independent Press* on 31 December 1818, which was amalgamated with the *Huntingdon, Bedford and Peterborough Gazette* in the following April, but was known as the *Cambridge Independent Press* from May 1839. Hatfield, like Flower, suffered for his liberal views. The tone of the paper is well exemplified in its report of the municipal inquiry of 1833, as contrasted with that of the *Chronicle*.

In January 1839 a third paper, the *Cambridge Advertiser*, appeared, which maintained an independent existence for over 25 years. The first daily, the *Cambridge Daily News*, issued from the offices of the *Cambridge Independent Press* in 1888, and in 1934 the *Independent* took over the *Chronicle* and became the sole Cambridge weekly. The printing department of the *Chronicle* survived as the St. Tibbs Press whilst the jobbing department of the *Independent Press* was taken over by Messrs. Heffers, who have a printing and publishing, in addition to their bookselling, establishment.

The book trade has flourished in Cambridge ever since John Siberch printed and sold the works of Erasmus. The market bookstalls of today, of which David's is the most famous, go back to the 16th century. The bookshops were mostly in the vicinity of Great St. Mary's, and in the 17th and 18th centuries were most numerous in the Regent Walk on the site of the present Senate House. The outstanding instance of continuity is No. 1 Trinity Street, which claims to be the oldest bookshop in England. The present building was erected about 1807, but the premises have been continuously occupied by booksellers since William Scarlett who was in business there at latest by 1594. John Nicholson, known like his father by the name of 'Maps', and A. D. Macmillan were 19th-century predecessors of Messrs. Bowes and Bowes who now occupy the site.

An analysis of employment in and around Cambridge in 1948 as compared with the same area in 1931 shows that the chief growth has been in government employment and in the manufacturing industries. Central government employment has risen by 350 per cent., and central and local government together now employ as many as do the University and the colleges. All manufacturing industries taken together have risen by 40 per cent. and the five manufacturing industry groups that have gained most have increased their employment by 180 per cent. Personal employment had fallen by 3,000, and the only other significant decline is that in the manufacture of clothing, which employed 521 as against 1,245. Apart from manufacture, the most notable advance was that of the building and decorating trades, where employment had risen from 3,099 to 4,483.

The causes for these striking 20th-century developments can be readily summarized. The introduction of motor bus services after 1918 has greatly enhanced the use of Cambridge as a county shopping centre. More than ever, it has become the focus of all kinds of county and regional activities. It has been the meeting-place of the Arts Council, the East Anglian Regional Hospital Board, the Traffic Commissioners for the Eastern Area, the Great Ouse Catchment Board, the National Farmers' Union, and the county political organizations. There is a large and growing airport on its outskirts. The temporary immigration resulting from the Second World War, the establishment of Cambridge as a regional governmental centre, with a large resident civil service, together with the restrictions imposed by law on the setting up of new industries in the London area have all contributed to the steep rise in the population curve. To the native amenities of a town with an exceptional combination of large open spaces, architectural and historical attractions and cultural opportunities Cambridge adds the advantage of being near enough to London to serve to some extent as a dormitory town.

Concern for the possible results of unregulated development led to the foundation in 1928 of the Cambridge Preservation Society which, in the best Cambridge tradition, embodied the joint concern of town, county, and University, the Mayor, the Lord Lieutenant, and the Vice-Chancellor being among its council members. Whilst failing to preserve the King's mill from destruction in 1928, the society has by purchase preserved other old buildings in the town and has averted disfiguring developments to the west and south of Cambridge, attracting, in addition to the donations and subscriptions of its own members, grants from the Pilgrim Trust.

David Mills

Town and Gown

Police, p. 77. Morals, p. 79. Theatres, p. 79. Health, p. 81. Jurisdiction, p. 81. Trade, p. 83. Finance, p. 84.

Both the economic and the constitutional development of Cambridge from the 13th to the 19th century were conditioned by the presence in the same town of 'two communities, the one of clerks, the other of laymen'. From the year 1231, when the birth of the two communities was registered by Henry III's command to the Mayor to appoint two burgesses to act with two masters of the University in fixing the rents of scholars' lodgings, the story of the relations of town and gown was one of endemic border warfare, with recurrent crises, the longest and fiercest being that under Elizabeth I. In the 18th century the warfare transformed itself into petty skirmishing, as administrative torpidity settled on both communities. It reopened in the 19th century with all the hostility and resentment that obsolete privilege and injured *amour-propre* can arouse. It was not until 1856 that peace was signed a peace that was 'lasting because there were no victors'.

Apart from general questions of precedence and prestige the main fields of conflict were those of police, morals and health, jurisdiction, trade and finance.

Police

As at Oxford, the coming of the clerks meant frequent brawls between students and townsmen and the appointment of a succession of judicial inquiries. The sheriff could be and was called by the Chancellor to enforce order, but after the charter of 1256 this might well be regarded as an infringement of the Borough's privileges, and in 1268 the responsibility for keeping the peace was definitely fixed on the townsmen. By a charter, modelled on that granted to Oxford in 1255, two aldermen and four senior burgesses were to be sworn to assist the Mayor and bailiffs in keeping the peace, to be assisted by two sworn men in each parish, who could assist both clerks and laymen. This did not satisfy the University; the burgesses were described as negligent and incompetent; and in April 1270 an agreement negotiated by the Lord Edward, and authenticated by the common seals of both parties as well as by the king's seal, established a system of joint responsibility. Every year, within a fortnight from the beginning of Michaelmas term, ten burgesses, seven from the town and three from the suburbs, together with five scholars from every English county, three from Scotland, two from Wales, and three from Ireland, were to be elected and sworn to keep the peace.

The clerks were to assist the burgesses in apprehending offenders cleric or lay; lists of heads of hostels and their inmates were to be kept; the lawless were to be expelled both from Borough and University and both parties alike were to swear to uphold the privileges of the University before proceeding to the elections. Thus was established the *Magna Congregatio* or Black Assembly in which the royal orders of 1231, 1268, and 1270 were carried out. The descriptions of 1421 and 1533 show how faithfully the forms were preserved. In 1533 the Assembly met in Great St. Mary's; the Mayor sat on the left hand of the Vice-Chancellor with the four bailiffs facing them, and the senior proctor administered the oath to the townsmen in English and to the scholars in Latin. The practical importance of the assembly was by now outweighed by its symbolical aspect. It was summoned and conducted by the Vice-Chancellor and it stood for the subordination of the town to the University. Both in 1546 and 1552 resentment was manifested by the burgesses. By 1668, when Alderman Newton described it, the Michaelmas paving leet had been amalgamated with it, and when the paving leet was superseded by the Improvement Commissioners in 1788 the Black Assembly ceased to be held.

Revived by a tactless Vice-Chancellor in 1817 it functioned for another 40 years for the presentment of nuisances and the swearing in of parish constables, but the scholars' obligation to swear to the peace had been completely forgotten. It enshrined the superiority of the University as much as the ceremony prescribed in the University's charter of 1317, whereby the Mayor and bailiffs on taking office had to swear to maintain the liberties of the University, informing the University officials in advance of time and place.

The Corporation was reprimanded for 'ungentle and perverse' attempts to escape the ceremony by Cromwell in 1537, by Somerset in 1551 and by Burleigh in 1596, and in 1597 the 'unreverent maner' of the Mayor was only endured by the Vice-Chancellor because of the multitude of townsmen in the town hall. In 1641 the Corporation decided to defy the University and in 1645 both parties petitioned Parliament. Though the Lords upheld the University, the town, represented in the Commons by Cromwell and Lowry, successfully continued their repudiation of the oath. The oath, however, was restored at the Restoration, and was only abolished, together with the Black Assembly, in 1856.

The University's duty of arresting persons who had infringed its regulations, whether a clerk who was devoting himself 'to misdeeds rather than to his studies', a bad character at Sturbridge fair, or a debtor, entailed the use of a prison, and as it had no right to have a gaol until 1603 it claimed the use first of the castle and later of the Tolbooth. In 1601 the University had obtained from the queen a 40-year lease of the Tolbooth, but the resulting lawsuit was decided in

January 1607 in favour of the town. Both town and gown were represented on the trust set up by Thomas Hobson in 1628 for building a workhouse and house of correction to be used by both authorities. The Spinning House, as it came to be called, ceased to be used by the town as a house of correction when the New Gaol was built, and was in effect the Vice-Chancellor's prison down to 1894.

The sharing of gaols led to trouble when townsmen were imprisoned by the ViceChancellor in the castle, outside the Borough boundary, or when town officials refused to commit prisoners or released them without warrant. Proctors acted concurrently with the town police and this joint responsibility occasionally created difficulties, as in 1559, when an attempt to carry out the advice of the county justices that 'the watches for the University and town of Cambridge should lovingly join together' during the time of Sturbridge Fair produced some free fights between the officials at midnight. The first responsibility for correcting nuisances presented in the leet lay with the town, but if they failed to act the University could take action after six weeks. In the 18th century notices about the enforcement of Acts of Parliament and other matters of public order were issued by Vice-Chancellor and Mayor jointly, the Vice-Chancellor's name always leading.

The charge to the Grand Jury at the Quarter Sessions for the town in October 1768 coupled the authority of the High Constable and the proctors, and stressed 'the necessity of a perfect union between the magistrates of the town and the University'. In 1833 the municipal commissioners, having themselves observed conditions on 5 November, found the town police very inefficient. They were told that the chief and high constables, 51 constables and 6 watchmen did far less to keep order in the town than the proctors and their servants, so that the condition of the town in the long vacation was scandalous. The powers of the Watch Committee set up under the Act of 1835 remained distinct from and unrelated to those of the proctors until 1856. The Watch Committee was, however, then reconstituted so as to contain five members of the Senate, appointed by the Senate, to sit with the ten town representatives.

Morals

The proctors, however, still retained the powers granted in 1317, and reinforced in 1561 and 1605, to expel common women from the town or suburbs and to search for, imprison, or banish such persons. Hobson's old workhouse had long served as a place of confinement for them by the name of the Spinning House. Powers once accepted as necessary for the protection of the morals of the undergraduates had by the second half of the 19th century come to be regarded as infringing the liberties of the subject, and in 1860 the summary arrest and commitment of five suspects led to a lawsuit that indicated the risks a proctor took in exercising these powers. For many years a policy of caution was pursued, but in February 1891 the rearrest of a girl who had escaped from the Spinning House produced an outcry in the press against the 'Academic Starchamber' and ten months later the University officials were convicted of carelessness and ignorance in the exercise of powers to which they were legally entitled by committing a highly dubious character without charging her properly. The inflamed feelings of the town were allayed largely by the good offices of the University members of the Borough Council, and after a series of conferences between town and gown both parties agreed in promoting the Cambridge University and Corporation Act of 1894 which provided for the concurrent action of the proctors and the town police in arresting loose women and the abolition of the Vice-Chancellor's jurisdiction over them, together with his veto on theatrical licences.

Theatres

Interference with the townsmen's diversions in the interests of the scholars only began in 1575, when the Privy Council instructed the Vice-Chancellor to prohibit 'pernicious and unhonest games' within five miles of the University. This was done mainly as a precaution against the plague, which was a serious interruption to studies. Games licensed by the county magistrates at the Howes were stopped in 1580, and football and bear-baiting at Chesterton in 1581, provoking protests from the Chesterton constables. In 1592 the prohibition of the showing of interludes and plays at the time of Sturbridge Fair began the long struggle over play-acting in and near Cambridge. The Corporation, which had been authorizing payments to minstrels and players for at least 100 years, and, in particular, since 1573, to the queen's players, naturally resented this, though the growing puritanism of the times may have diminished the grievance. James I's charter to the University gave the Vice-Chancellor full powers to prohibit all idle games and diversions within five miles of the town, and to expel all actors, jugglers, rope-dancers, and such, and forbade the licensing or toleration of them.

In spite of this the town erected a bull ring on Peas Hill in 1604, which was still there in 1662. When in 1701 the Corporation licensed the performance of plays at Sturbridge Fair the University constituted an *ad hoc* police of 62 M.A.s to enforce discipline and the Vice-Chancellor ordered the theatre booth to be demolished and the actor Dogget to be imprisoned. This did not end the matter; Joseph Kettle, one of the county magistrates, built a permanent theatre on his own land in the suburbs, and petitions from him and from town and county residents for dramatic entertainments during Sturbridge Fair and from the University for the retention of its privileges were heard in Parliament in April 1737. The rights of the University were upheld in the Players and Tavern Act of June 1737; all producers of plays in the precincts of Oxford or Cambridge were to be deemed rogues and vagabonds, but the Vice-Chancellor, though empowered to punish, was not forbidden to license performances.

There was much theatrical activity in Norwich and a circuit system was gradually developed with a touring company allowing three weeks for a visit to Sturbridge Fair each autumn. By 1748 a dramatic performance in September had become the established practice, and as the century went on, the three weeks' season was a great social function enjoyed by town and gown alike. Players from Covent Garden as well as Norwich attended; benefit performances for the Cambridge charity schools were given; and three permanent buildings in succession were erected in Barnwell. The fact, however, that for the rest of the year there was no theatre in Cambridge was, as the 18th-century guide-books pointed out, one of the drawbacks of residence there.

The Act for regulating theatres in 1843 extended the Vice-Chancellor's veto to a radius of fourteen miles, covering Newmarket and St. Ives. Under the award of 1856 all dramatic performances were licensed by both Mayor and Vice-Chancellor, but by 1894 this had become such an empty form that the University was willing to surrender it. Meanwhile the theatre had not always prospered in Cambridge. In 1853 the Lyceum Company played for twelve nights, in 1858 the London Opera Company came for a week, and in 1861 and 1867 the London Royal English Opera Company played for short seasons. The theatre season usually covered August and September with programmes ranging from low comedy to grand opera and Shakespeare. The Barnwell Theatre Royal, rebuilt in 1816, flourished for many years, but in the mid-century, although Charles Dickens gave some readings there, dramas gave way to panoramas, and finally the theatre after serving as a mission hall was deserted.

In 1926 this theatre was said to be the oldest surviving in the British Isles, when Mr. Terence Gray reopened it as the Festival Theatre 'in order that it might become a centre for the practice of the most advanced stage craft in the country, a sort of university of dramatic art'. The Festival opened with the *Oresteia* of Aeschylus translated by R. C. Trevelyan, and its brilliant experimental programmes went on until 1934. Regular productions ceased in 1940.

Meanwhile the other Cambridge theatre owed its origin to an amateur dramatic club, the Bijou, formed about 1875 by William Beales Redfern. Redfern bought St. Andrew's Hall in St. Andrew's Street, and in 1896 he rebuilt the hall as the New Theatre. His enterprise was strongly supported by John Willis Clark, the University Registrary, who was a director of the New Theatre Company from the beginning, and in 1902 succeeded Redfern as its chairman, a post which he retained until his death in 1910. The first production was that of *Hamlet* by the Haymarket Theatre Company.

The last theatre to be built in Cambridge is the Arts, opened in 1936 in Peas Hill, and owing its existence very largely to the efforts of John Maynard Keynes. As bursar of King's College Keynes was able to help with the provision of a site. He also contributed generously with his advice and his money. In the early years he acted as business manager, and even on occasion sold tickets at the box office. The theatre has never had a repertory company. Its policy is to depend on visiting companies, and to try to provide the best of all kinds of drama.

Apart from the Bijou a number of amateur dramatic clubs have contributed to the theatrical history of Cambridge. The Garrick Club, formed in 1834, gave performances at Barnwell Theatre Royal, but was disbanded in 1842. The Amateur Dramatic Club, formed in 1855, has flourished for more than a century. Its founder was F. C. Burnand, later editor of *Punch*. It secured permanent premises by the Hoop Brewery in Jesus Lane and was at times rather a social than a dramatic club. After a fire in 1933 the premises were rebuilt with a theatre seating 200. The Footlights, another University dramatic society, was formed in 1883, and several of its members have subsequently made the stage their profession. The Rodney Club began to give annual performances in 1889, first at the A.D.C. theatre in Jesus Lane, later at the Barnwell Theatre Royal, and since 1936 at the Arts. It has its own small theatre seating 80, at 148 Chesterton Road. The Marlowe Dramatic Society, formed to perform *Faustus* in 1908, with Rupert

Brooke as its president and Geoffrey Keynes as its secretary, has since produced an Elizabethan play each year. Finally the Mummers, formed in 1926, to include members of the women's colleges, gives two performances each year.

Health

The University, though necessarily concerned for the health of its members, never claimed an independent jurisdiction in matters of health and sanitation. Under the royal charter of 1268 it held that the town was bound to keep Cambridge properly paved, cleaned, and drained, and complaints about failure to perform these duties in 1330 and 1351 were followed in 1391 by an order to the Vice-Chancellor to act with the Mayor in enforcing the recent Statute of Cambridge. Power to inquire into nuisances was given to the Vice-Chancellor in 1459, and the indenture of 1503, revised in 1575, provided that he could take action on presentments after six weeks if the Mayor had done nothing. The Paving Act of 1544 fixed joint responsibility on University and town for the cleanliness of Cambridge, and set up the machinery which endured until 1788 for dealing with local amenities. As will be seen below, the ViceChancellor took an active and sometimes a leading part in these concerns, Addenbrooke's Hospital being the most outstanding example of the fruitful co-operation of town and gown for the bodily welfare of Cambridge.

Jurisdiction

The jurisdiction of the University over its own members when they only were involved was a matter of course in the Middle Ages: conflict of jurisdiction only arose when laymen were involved, for the townsmen could assert their own chartered right to answer in their own courts. Under the University's charter of 1268 the Chancellor could claim the person of a clerk who had attacked a layman, and in 1305 he was given power to cite burgesses and other laymen to answer scholars in all personal actions. In 1317 these were particularized as cases concerning loans, the leasing of houses, the hire, sale, or loan of horses, cloth or victuals and all other contracts concerning movables. The Chancellor was further empowered to commit laymen as well as clerks to the castle for bodily violence. In protesting against these privileges the burgesses alleged, in 1337, that under this system laymen injuring clerks were punished and clerks injuring laymen were liberated without making amends, and that scholars purchased debts and contracts and sued for them in the University courts where they might be tried by civil and not common law.

The town ordinance of 1403 which forbade burgesses to sue before the Chancellor concerning contracts which could be determined before the Mayor and bailiffs suggests that some preferred this procedure. But the jurisdiction of the University was not restricted; it was further enlarged by the addition of stationers, writers, bookbinders, and illuminators to the persons whose trespasses were justiciable by the Chancellor, while the charter of 1383 added scholars' servants and University employees to the list. The agreement of 1503 added apothecaries, physicians, surgeons, barbers, and parchment makers, and was endorsed with the names of some 70 persons coming within these categories. At the same time, the procedure by which persons claiming privilege were to be handed over to the University authorities in St. Mary's Church was exactly defined. In 1589 the 'privileged persons' were declared to include the servants and children of all married graduates living in the town, all gardeners, butchers, barbers, and brewers of every college or hall, the husbands of college laundresses, the keeper of the University library, the University printer, the University plumber, and 'the man who times the University clock'. This concession was part of the price paid by the town for securing its rights to Sturbridge Fair; but Nicholas Gaunt, the Mayor who assented to 'these new jurisdictions of the University', was regarded as a traitor, and, as John Wickstede put it, 'having been put out of his Aldermanship lived the remainder of his life in gout, want and misery and hateful to all the townsmen'.

It is not surprising that bad feeling between the two communities mounted. Privilege had its financial aspect; members of the University were forbidden to be burgesses, and the townsmen complained in

1596 that as many as eleven score graduates were making their livelihood by husbandry, brewing or other trades, and yet escaping payment of the subsidies though they outnumbered the 'subsidy men' in the town. Such residents, in no sense scholars, were exempt from the jurisdiction, routine duties, and common charges of the Borough.

Jurisdiction in matters of trade, conferred on the University in 1382, added thenceforth to the causes of friction. By the agreement of 1503 the Mayor was to have jurisdiction in victualling pleas when a burgess was plaintiff, and the Chancellor when a 'foreigner' was plaintiff; the Mayor was to have jurisdiction over wholesale transactions, unless a clerk was a party.

There were several cases of the vindication of University privilege in the 17th century, but by the 18th the claim of cognizance was becoming anachronistic. The town bench, which included both University and Borough magistrates, were allowed to hear doubtful cases, and 'privileged persons' who preferred the lay courts were no longer penalized. In 1771, in a case of assault by two scholars on a printer, the University put in a claim, but abandoned it with little protest. As Soame Jenyns wrote to Hardwicke, 'these separate jurisdictions, where there is no trial by jury, are contrary to the spirit of our present constitution'. Probably the last claim of cognizance by the Vice-Chancellor was made and disallowed in the Borough court in 1844, whilst the jurisdiction over weights and measures, regrators and victuals, still being exercised in the same decade at Sturbridge, Midsummer and Reach Fairs in the Commissary's court, was abolished by agreement in the Act of 1856. The jurisdiction of the Vice-Chancellor's Court was then confined to cases in which both parties were members of the University.

Trade

A University had to protect its scholars against high prices and poor quality; and in accordance with established University custom the writ of 1231 instructed the two authorities each to appoint two taxors to fix jointly the rents of scholars' lodgings. Very soon the co-operation of the Chancellor was required for the holding of the assize of bread and ale. The Borough, however, retained effective control until February 1382, when the assize of bread, wine, and beer was granted wholly and for ever to the University, with the custody of weights and measures and the cognizance of forestalling and regrating. This grant was expressly declared to cover Sturbridge Fair. The restoration of the town's liberties, saving those of the University, in May 1382, established a joint supervision of town trade and set up causes of friction that continued from 1384 to 1856. In 1554, for instance, the town complained of the too liberal interpretation of the grant of 1382 to cover the enforcement of later statutes, in particular University interference with the licensing of alehouses. Elizabeth I's charter to the University, however, confirmed its right to enforce statutes, and to act as the sole clerk of the market in Sturbridge Fair. Though town and gown could co-operate against the pewterers of London, and the townsmen supported the University in dealing with the brewers of Cambridge, Sturbridge Fair, in which the burgesses had the monopoly of holding booths, and from which the Corporation drew large profits, was inevitably a source of friction.

From 1553 to 1589 the town was making persistent attempts to get the fair into its own hands. It nearly succeeded in 1558, when the Provost of King's dissuaded the University from selling its rights. Even when in 1589 the town had secured the lordship of the fair, there was still an overlap of functions. As the fair dwindled in importance, however, this became less irksome than the question of licensing. In 1564 the Chancellor's right to license alehouses had been explicitly approved by the queen and in 1597 the University reduced their number from 80 to 30 whilst its right to license vintners was vindicated against Raleigh as well as the town. All Cambridge inns had to obtain the Vice-Chancellor's licence, and the rights of the University were upheld, against protest, in the Act of 1737.

The town had, by the composition of 1503, accepted the right of the University to control the retail trade in victuals; in 1532 there were complaints about its slackness in enforcing the assize. When the grant had first been made, the townsmen said, the scholars had lived in small halls, and bought their bread and ale of the poor inhabitants of the town; now that the colleges were becoming wealthy, they had their own brew- houses and bakehouses, and cared little about breaches of the assize, accepting bribes from the offenders. The University responded with new regulations; and a century later the Mayor and town magistrates reported to the Privy Council that they left the enforcing of the assize and the punishment of forestallers and the like to the University officials.

Various acts of Parliament, from 1710 to 1824, confirmed the right of the University to fix the price and weight of bread, rights exercised by the Vice-Chancellor and proctors until the abolition of the Assize of Bread in 1836. The rapid rise of prices led to the revival of the University's power to punish regrators and forestallers in 1792; poultry, dairy produce, and vegetables were not to be sold in Cambridge market for re-sale before noon. Riots in 1795 led to collaboration between Mayor and Vice-Chancellor to deal with the price of butchers' meat, and again in 1800 they acted together.

By the middle of the 19th century the University rights of regulating trade had come to be regarded as obsolete and annoying. Since 1836 the town magistrates had been able to license alehouses, and new powers had been given to the Mayor by the Act of 1850 for regulating markets and fairs, but the rights of the University had still been reserved. The memorial drawn up for the town in 1852 urged that the concurrent licensing of alehouses by town and University and the sale of vintners' licences for profit was undesirable; and that the supervision of weights and measures by the University taxors, still the sole authority, was inefficient. It also objected to the practice of discommuning. This practice, whereby members of the University were forbidden to deal with a specific Cambridge tradesman, had come into use in the 16th century, and served as a good working substitute for the power of excommunication as exercised against Mayors in 1524 and 1529 and abandoned in 1533. It had been an effective and unpopular weapon in the war of town and gown. By the award of 1856 the University retained this right as well as that of licensing vintners, though the right to license alehouses was surrendered. In abolishing the taxors, who had acted as the agents of the University in supervising prices since 1231, with one brief interval from 1541 to 1546, the Act of 1856 wound up a very long story.

Finance

Whilst both trade and justice had their financial aspects, participation in the financial burdens of the town formed a distinct issue. From 1496 at least the lands of the colleges and the goods of the individual members of the University had been exempted normally from both lay and clerical subsidies. In 1596, as stated above, the town had expressed its resentment at the large number of tax-free hangers-on of the University. With the introduction of a poor rate the preferential treatment of college and University property was further emphasized;

University and college property were not assessed to parochial rates, though the University made a voluntary contribution, fixed at £120 in 1650, on the condition that the streets were kept free from beggars.

This contribution was ultimately raised to £240. The charter of 1632, in giving the Borough power to levy rates for supporting the burdens of the Borough on residents as well as burgesses, exempted scholars and privileged persons from payment. On the imposition of the Land Tax in 1700 the sites of the colleges and the stipends of University officers were again exempted, but the University undertook to contribute roughly 1/9 of the total amount imposed on the town and University. From 1718 onwards the payments were falling into arrears, and a crisis was produced by the acquisition of the Senate House in 1722, which suddenly raised the charge upon the parishioners of Great St. Mary's. The parishioners, the town, and the University petitioned Parliament, and by an agreement of the following year, confirmed by Parliament, the ratio of £50 to £1,423 was accepted for the University's quota.

Thus in 1854 the University was paying £100 to the town's £2,700. This was not so inequitable as it might seem, since the assessment allowed for the exemption of college sites. On the other hand the University accepted responsibility for 2/5 of the total amount leviable by the improvement commissioners under the Act of 1788 for the expenses of paving, lighting, and cleaning the town, a proportion which by 1854 had become excessive owing to the growth of the inhabited area.

The fact that the University made no contribution to the expenses of maintaining the police force set up in 1836 under the Municipal Corporations Act was also an issue. A proposal in 1847 to make a voluntary contribution was rejected in the non-Regent House by a narrow majority, and a negotiated agreement between the two parties that the University should contribute one-third of the expense and have representation on the Watch Committee was similarly rejected, by a large majority, in 1850. By the award of 1856, however, all outstanding financial issues were settled. The Land Tax assessment remained unchanged; all University property except the Senate House, the library, the schools and lecture-rooms, the laboratories and museums, and the college chapels and libraries was made taxable; the contribution under the Improvement Acts was altered from $2/5$ to $¼$ and the University was given five representatives on the Watch Committee.

¶In the long rivalry of town and gown, ushered in by the disorders caused by the lawless young clerks of the 13th century, as the wealth and privileges of the University and its colleges increased, the weight of the royal power had been, almost invariably, thrown on its side. The charter of 1317, establishing the formal precedence of the University by the annual ceremony of the Mayor's oath, irritated civic susceptibilities, and, in spite of friendliness between individuals, and the foundation of a college by the town guilds, the resentment of the townsmen exploded in 1381, with the destruction of University muniments and the extortion of wholesale renunciation of college and University privilege by sealed deeds.

The resulting punishment added the further injury of the University's supervision of the markets, and the revival of prosperity after the 15th century regression produced an endless succession of statements of grievances from both parties, with appeals to the noble patrons; to the Lady Margaret, to the Protector Somerset, Chancellor of the University and High Steward of the town; to Thomas Cromwell; to Lord North; and above all to Burghley, in his two-fold position of chief minister of the Crown and Chancellor of the University.

Fuller is probably right in connecting the increase of friction with the Reformation. A succession of com- positions allayed but did not eliminate the irritation. The University's request for representation in Parliament, first put forward in 1570 and granted finally in 1604, was the outcome of fear and distrust of the town. The town countered in 1616 by petitioning for the title and status of a city. The University urged that this would endanger their privileges, and James refused the petition, asserting that 'the home of the Muses could gain no additional honour from the plebeian title of city'. The national contest of the 17th century added a religious and political flavour to the old conflict, and the puritanical and parliamentary town had for the moment the advantage over the Anglican and royalist University and could defy it with impunity.

But in 1660 the tables were turned; and in the comparative calm of the 18th century the University, always solicitous for the health and amenities of Cambridge, was actually making good some of the administrative derelictions of the torpid Corporation. Benthamite reform, however, which revolutionized the Borough government, left the University untouched, and the revival of bad feeling in the first half of the 19th century was largely attributable to survivals or even revivals of out-dated privilege. It was a triumph of common sense over feeling when, in 1855, direct negotiations having broken down, town and gown as in 1270, in 1503, and 1526 and 1548, agreed to refer the points at issue to an arbitrator and Sir John Patteson's award was embodied in the Act of 5 June 1856.

Though peace was signed there was still a barrier between the two communities. Members of the University could not hold office or vote in municipal elections. Not until 1889 was partnership in the government of Cambridge effected. By an Act of 1889 implementing the Local Government Act of 1888 two members of the Borough Council were to be annually appointed by the Senate, and four others elected by the colleges. As subsequently modified, this means that in the City council of 1951 two aldermen and six councillors represented the University. Beginning with Horace Darwin in 1896, a succession of University aldermen have held the mayoralty of Cambridge, and since 1907 their wives also have served on the council and its committees.

Public Health

In tracing the history of health in Cambridge we are once more confronted by the two characteristic governing motifs: geography and the presence of the University. Harrison said in 1577 'Cambridge standeth very well, save that it is somewhat low and near to the Fens, whereby the wholesomeness of the air there is not a little corrupted', and the very slight elevation above sea-level makes the disposal of refuse by water a serious problem. From the first coming of the clerks, the concern of the University for the health of its members has acted as a stimulus to raise hygienic standards, and has led to much fruitful co-operation between the two communities.

From an early date town sanitation was associated with the town ditch. Though its origin is undoubtedly far earlier, the first official reference to it is Henry III's order of 20 February 1268, 'That the town be cleansed from dirt and filth; that the watercourse should be opened and kept open as of old so that the filth may run off; and that the great ditch of the town be cleansed.' Already in 1268, it would seem, 'What was meant for fortifying had become a great annoying.'

The town records show that it was used as a receptacle for all kinds of refuse entrails, dung, and garbage; privies, 'seges', or 'bocards' were built over it. Six loads of manure were carted away from it in 1522 when a culvert was built at the point where Jesus Lane crossed it. A survey of the ground levels explains its stagnancy.

There was a slight natural fall from Barnwell Gate in both directions which made through scouring impossible. The tradition that it was the holding of Parliament at Cambridge that produced the first Health Act in 1388 is supported by the terms of the statute referring to the casting of various 'corruptions' into ditches and rivers, and imposing on the Mayors and bailiffs the duty of cleaning up their towns on pain of answering for neglect in Chancery. The machinery for enforcing these regulations was gradually built up, Mayor and Chancellor being stimulated by commands from Westminster. By-laws were reinforced by the annual proclamation for the 'avoydance of muck' and from 1459 both Vice-Chancellor and Mayor were empowered to inquire in their leets into such nuisances as wandering hogs, highway dunghills, the defilement of the town ditch and ill-paved roads. The co-operation of the two was registered in the indenture of 1503, which is in effect a local sanitary code, and was revised and renewed in 1575.

The primary responsibility rested with the town, but if the Mayor failed to take action upon a presentment within six weeks the Vice-Chancellor was to act. In 1544 an Act promoted by the Borough

Members of Parliament set up the machinery by which for the next 240 years Cambridge amenities were supposed to be guarded; the establishment of the paving leet held jointly by Mayor and Chancellor for enforcing the householder's statutory responsibility for paving the roadway in front of his house, for cleansing the streets, and for dealing with nuisances in general.

Conditions favourable to the pollution of wells and the breeding of sewer rats were promoted by the overcrowding of the 16th and 17th centuries; from 1584 onward the central government exhorted Mayor and Chancellor to check the practice of subdividing tenements to the overburdening of the town, 'a thing dangerous in time of infection'. The pestilence of 1348–9 ushered in 300 years of similar recurrent visitations. Between 1510 and 1550 there was an epidemic, on the average, every three years; between 1630 and 1645 there were nine. University activities were suspended 28 times, and even Sturbridge Fair was cancelled repeatedly.

The death roll ranged from over 429 in 1610 to 797 in 1666. Measures for dealing with it were gradually worked out, the justices of the peace assisting the corporation officials. Perfume, frankincense, charcoal and juniper, pitch and resin were used for 'ayringe and sweetninge' the Town Hall or churches where assemblies met. Suspected victims were systematically 'searched'. Infected houses were closed. Makeshift isolation hospitals were put up at the old clay pits, now Gonville Place, on Midsummer Common, Jesus Green, or Coldham's Common. These finally gave place to permanent pest houses, completed, ironically enough, in 1666. They were pulled down in 1703. Vivid descriptions of plague conditions, mostly by members of the University, survive for 1625, 1630, 1636, and 1665.

The visitation of 1573 produced not only the reissue in 1575 of the street-cleaning indenture, but proposals for a new water-supply. In November 1574 the Vice-Chancellor, in a letter to Burghley admitting 'our synnes' as the principal cause of the plague, noted as a 'secondarie cause' the corruption of the King's Ditch, and suggested 'that the water that cometh from Shelford to Trumpington ford might be conveighed to the King's Ditch for the perpetual scouringe of the same, the which would be a singular benefite for the healthsomenes both of the Universite and of the Towne'.

He enclosed a map marked with the proposed course of the conduit, but the matter rested for 30 years. At last in 1606 a number of undertakers, including the University carrier Hobson, subscribed towards the project. A commission of sewers was appointed in 1608, and after a hortatory letter from James I and some compulsory purchases of land, an indenture was drawn up in 1610. By this deed, our chief evidence on the project, Thomas Chaplyn, the lord of the manor of Trumpington, granted to the town and University a 1,000-year lease of the land through which the recently-made watercourse was to convey a current of water from Nine Wells at White Hill near Shelford 'to scour and cleanse the common drain or sewer called the King's Ditch, as well as for the commodity of sundry drains and watercourses belonging to divers colleges'. In the last clause lay the weakness of the scheme.

The stream that can be seen today flowing down Trumpington Street in two small rivulets into the ditch under Mill Lane had six divergent branches. It supplied water not only to the fountain in the marketplace, completed in 1614, with which Hobson's name was especially associated, but also to the 'Red Lion' in the Petty Cury, to a bath in Pembroke College, and to ponds in Emmanuel and Christ's College grounds. The force of the flow was dissipated, the King's Ditch remained imperfectly scoured, and the plague recurred with increasing violence. As a supply of drinking-water the 'new river' was a welcome addition to the medieval fountain that had given its name to Conduit Street. The Franciscans, about 1327, had conveyed the water from Madingley Road to their house on the site of Sidney Sussex College.

The trust was endowed by legacies of land and money from several persons, including Hobson himself and Stephen Perse. Its income in 1950 was just under £300, and it still maintains the conduit though this is now only ornamental. The fountain in Trinity Great Court, as well as the taps inside the hall and outside the Great Gate, are still supplied from the same source as the Franciscans used. The town pumps, drawing from shallow wells, often supplied polluted water; three at least adjoined overloaded churchyards.

The King's Ditch gradually disappeared underground. By 1574 it was covered over in Mill Lane and part of Pembroke Street; in 1688 in Walls Lane . In 1798 Sidney ditch was covered in. In 1815 it was considered most unlikely that 'a very ancient sewer called the King's Ditch, and for the most part covered in' could have contributed to the epidemic of that year. The remaining uncovered portions in Park Street, Tibbs Row, and the Botanical Garden on the site of the Austin Friars were built over in the 19th century; the ditch can still be located under the science laboratories.

In 1815 it was supposed that the 'proper persons' would take steps to remove any obstruction in the ancient sewer that might cause trouble; but those proper persons were no longer the Corporation. As in many other localities, an authority had been constituted by Act of Parliament to see to the health and amenities for which the town government had in effect abandoned all responsibility. As the population increased and standards rose, conditions deteriorated, and the state of the roads was a public scandal. Gunning's description of Trumpington Street, with the channel of running water dividing the road into two unequal parts, has often been cited. From 1769 onwards, when Tunwell's efforts met with violent opposition, attempts were being made to establish a statutory authority.

Finally in 1788 an Act was passed which superseded that of 1544. It created a body of Paving Commissioners, who were empowered to pave, light, and cleanse the town, and to levy rates for those purposes. Seventeen were nominated in the Act; the remaining 52 were to be elected by the Corporation, the University, and the 14 parishes of Cambridge. In 1794 18 more representatives of the University and 14 more of the parishes were added, bringing the number up to 99.

From 1788 to 1889 the Improvement Commissioners were responsible for the lighting, paving, and drainage of Cambridge. A new lighting system was installed in 1788, the central gutter in Trumpington Street was replaced by two roadside runnels, and the repaving of the town was completed by 1793.

The 'Cambridge fever' of January to April 1815, probably typhoid, called attention to health conditions. The population had been increasingly rapidly, and though the Inclosure Acts of 1801, 1802, and 1807 had relieved the congestion, and Cambridge was said to be 'famed for its salubrity', housing conditions were very bad and sanitation non-existent in the older parishes inside the ditch. In 1848, at the request of the ratepayers, Cambridge was constituted a district under the Public Health Act of that year, and the Improvement Commissioners were recognized as the Local Board of Health. The report, published in May 1849, of the General Board's Inspector into the sewerage, drainage, water-supply, and health of the town gives a terrible picture of the overcrowding and filth in the small courts.

Some of these were only 2½ feet across, sun and air were excluded, and the only recent advance in sanitation that could be recorded was that the scavengers' carts came thrice instead of twice a week to collect the 'night soil'. 'The conditions are so wretched as to be a disgrace to civilization; it is next to impossible for the inhabitants to be healthy, cleanly, moral, decent or modest.' Some had to go a quarter of a mile to obtain clean water; others paid a farthing a gallon for it. 'There are no public baths; the inhabitants have no resource but the sluggish and polluted Cam.' Six hundred and twenty-five thousand gallons of water a day were needed for the town. Slaughterhouse offal in what is now Corn Exchange Street and a horrible dump of old bones in East Street 'in the midst of dwelling houses' are also described. On the other hand, Cambridge was commended for its new burial grounds and for its open spaces, especially Parker's Piece.

The census of 1851 reported the demolition of old tenements as well as the clearance due to the fire of 1849 in the Market Place, but the opening up of the old yards and courts is best followed in the maps of the town. A fresh-water supply was obtained from Cherry Hinton in 1855, later supplemented from wells at Fulbourn and from Shardelowes near the Fleam Dyke. Its exceptionally pure water-supply has never been known to fail, even in the driest summer. The foundation at this time of the Cambridge University and Town Water Company was one of the most important events in the sanitary history of the town. It now serves a very wide area, including much more than the City.

From 1864 onwards the question of a main drainage system was under hot discussion, schemes being propounded in 1864, 1866, 1870, 1871, and 1886. The Rivers Pollution Act of 1876 made it more difficult, as the growth of the town made more unpleasant the use of the Cam for sewer outfalls. The Bursar of Trinity in 1884, one of the Improvement Commissioners since 1869, could say that 'a sweet pellucid stream was from a sanitary point of view more a luxury than a necessity'. It had been felt for some time that the health authority was out of date. As remodelled after the Local Government Act of 1835, it consisted of 88 members, 9 *ex officio*, 36 elected by the University and 43 by the Corporation and the 14 vestries; the quorum was seven. Under the provisions of the Public Health Act of 1875 the Improvement Commissioners eventually ceased to exist. Their powers were handed over to the Town Council on 9 November 1889, and it was a new health authority that carried through the main drainage system in 1895. This solved the problem of the levels by a system of deep sewers and a pumping station two miles from the centre of the town.

The responsibility once incumbent on the Mayor and the Vice-Chancellor and later on the Improvement Commissioners, with the additional functions necessitated by modern demands, are today discharged by the various sub-committees of the City Council, whilst the Conservators of the Cam, appointed by City, University, and county, are still responsible for wider ranging drainage. As in the field of education and juvenile employment, the municipal authorities have profited by the work and the experience of earlier voluntary welfare agencies, sometimes taking over their functions and sometimes, as in the field of housing, working alongside. Amongst these, special reference should be made to the results accomplished for the health of the mothers and children of Cambridge.

The survey of social conditions in Cambridge published in 1908 reports that in 1904, 107 infants under twelve months died in Cambridge roughly one in eight; in 1949, with a considerably increased population, the number was 35, or one in 38. For this the Voluntary Association for Maternity and Child Welfare was very largely responsible. It originated in the appointment, in 1906, of two health visitors to mothers in their homes, by a society formed to combat tuberculosis. In 1910 a milk depot was set up in Newmarket Road, to which babies were brought to be weighed, and by 1912 there were four infant welfare centres. In 1915 the association was formally constituted.

From 1917 an annual grant was made to it by the Borough, and in 1919 the Borough Council requested the Voluntary Association to organize all the work, now very extensive, with the financial backing of the town. In 1937 the association, at its own request, surrendered the responsibility to the Maternity and Child Welfare Committee, with which it had been linked since 1919, but it continued to organize voluntary help at the centres till the end of the war, and only wound itself up in 1946. Cambridge was, in 1909, the first town in the British Isles to give dental treatment for school children. Here also the pioneer work had been on a voluntary basis.

In 1815 it was claimed that 'patients in the last stage of a decline have recovered on coming to reside here', and it may be that the open spaces even then counteracted the sunless and noisome yards. In 1949 it was as true as it had been in 1925 to say that 'Cambridge is among the healthiest of the larger towns in England'.

Of the medieval hospitals, St. John's was for the poor rather than the sick. Sturbridge leper hospital ceased for lack of patients and that of St. Anthony and St. Eloy became an almshouse, as has been told elsewhere. They were both outside the town ditch and the second, commemorated today in St. Anthony Street and St. Eligius Street, gave to the suburb outside Trumpington Gate the name of the Spittle End. It is a remarkable fact that a site so near by should have been chosen in the 18th century for Addenbrooke's Hospital.

Addenbrooke's Hospital

John Addenbrooke, a fellow of St. Catharine's College and a Cambridge M.D., practised medicine in London for a short time after leaving Cambridge in 1711 and died at Buntingford in 1719. He left his books and his medicine chest to St. Catharine's, and bequeathed the reversion of the small fortune he had inherited from his mother's brother 'to hire, fit up or purchase or erect a building fit for a small physical hospital in the town of Cambridge for poor people, to be open to every sick poor person of any county, if room and revenue permitted'.

Mrs. Addenbrooke died in 1720, but financial and legal difficulties impeded action until in 1759 Chancery appointed eleven new trustees, of whom ten were heads of Cambridge colleges. These purchased in 1763 the present site in Trumpington Street, then almost at the southern extremity of the town, and building began. By 1766 £4,000 had been spent and only £200 remained to build a kitchen and provide for staff and upkeep. On 30 April 1766 a meeting of the gentlemen of the University, the county, and the Borough was held, and a scheme was approved for a hospital based on the joint-stock principle prevalent in 18th-century philanthropy.

Immediate subscriptions enabled the hospital to open on 13 October 1766, and an Act of Parliament of 1767 empowered Addenbrooke's trustees to make over their funds and responsibilities to a corporation consisting of *ex-officio* officers representing the University, the county, and the Borough, life-governors who had made a donation of 20 guineas upwards, and annual subscribers of 2 guineas upwards. A private infirmary was thus constituted a 'general hospital'. The Lord Lieutenant was the *ex-officio* president, and there are frequent references to the running of the hospital in the seventies and eighties in the letters of Dr. Ewin, the first treasurer, and Dr. Plumptre to Lord Hardwicke.

Though Addenbrooke had set no geographical limits, the rules drawn up for the hospital secured that normally only poor Cambridgeshire patients should be received. Three Cambridge parishes appear on the first subscription list, and three county parishes in 1768; by 1803 all the Borough parishes and 52 country parishes were subscribers, of which six were in adjoining counties. In the first year 106 in-patients and 157 out-patients were treated; the average annual number of in-patients rose from 282, 1770–9 to 379, 1780–9, but fell to 333 in the next decade. The average number of out-patients rose in the same period from 324 to 376. Infectious and incurable patients were not received and patients were normally discharged after two months.

The subscribers' governing rights were exercised by a quorum of nine in quarterly general courts at which appointments were made, accounts passed, contracts approved and rules revised, whilst a weekly board, with a quorum of five, regulated the admission of patients and dealt with current business. Town, county, and University co-operated in steady support, and two prominent members of the anti-Mortlock faction in the Corporation served the hospital long and faithfully, Alderman Newling as treasurer from 1770 to 1815 and Alderman Bond as a visiting surgeon from 1775 to 1803.

In addition to subscriptions, donations, and legacies, the hospital funds were augmented by collections taken at the annual sermon at Commencement and the proceeds of benefit concerts then held, but these were uncertain sources, and it was reported in 1802 that for the last seven years expenses had exceeded receipts by about £150. The weekly meetings had been poorly attended, and the leading members of the medical and administrative staff had held their posts for 25 years or more. Reforms were obviously needed, and eighteen select governors were appointed who undertook to attend the weekly boards in rotation. These persons served in effect as executive and finance committee until 1898, though any governor was still free to attend the meetings. A financial drive increased the subscribers from 526 to 728, and brought in some 1,200 new donations, whilst the institution of 'Hospital Sunday' in some 119 parish churches provided a fresh source of revenue.

The expansion of the hospital proceeded rapidly. By the middle of the 19th century the average number of in-patients per annum had reached 690, by 1880, 880, by 1900, 1,320. The number of beds, about

100 in 1866, was 153 in 1889. In the latter year the hospital contained three surgical and three medical wards, two eye wards, two children's wards, an accident ward, and three special wards. By 1915 the number of beds had reached 192 and in 1951, 357.

In 1822 two wings and a colonnade were added, masking but not replacing the original building which remains today embedded in the modern structure. The extension had been made possible by the legacy of £7,000 from John Bowtell, the antiquary and a native of Cambridge, in 1813. The hospital was greatly enlarged in 1864–5, a third story being added. New wards were built in 1878, a dormitory in 1883, an outpatients department and a nurses' building in 1895–6, a clinical laboratory in 1913, new wards in 1915, 1929, and 1932, and an additional home for the nursing staff in 1924, and new accommodation for the orthopaedic department and the medical staff in 1934.

After the reforms of 1802 no change of importance was made in the government of the hospital until 1898, though the rules were revised in 1812 and 1833. By 1898 the need of change was felt both on administrative and financial grounds. The quarterly courts were out of date, especially in relation to appointments, and rival schemes were hotly discussed by the governors. A committee of twelve, representing University, town, and county, was appointed to consider the situation. The proposal to delegate the government of the hospital to an advisory council of fifteen governors was rejected in favour of a more elaborate scheme which was examined and approved by the Charity Commissioners, and incorporated in the Addenbrooke's Hospital Scheme Confirmation Act of 1903.

On 12 March 1910 a meeting of representative working men was held at the hospital, at which it was decided to establish a system of regular contributions to a fund for maintaining the hospital. This scheme functioned as the Cambridge and District Workers' Hospital Fund until 1931. It then became the Contributory Scheme under which the various county parishes, like those of the Borough, secured for their inhabitants rights to be received in sickness in return for a standing subscription, a system which continued until the passing of the National Health Act of 1948.

In 1767 the resident medical staff consisted of one apothecary, who was expected to be permanently on the premises. His salary rose from £25 with a bonus of £5 in 1770 to £50 without a bonus in 1800. In 1846 it was £86. He then had a dispenser to assist him and an apprentice whose premium augmented his income. The matron's salary was £15 in 1770 and had risen to £50 by 1833, but her responsibility was merely that of a housekeeper and cook, with some disciplinary duties added. In 1800 she had four assistant nurses whose combined salaries came to £38. There were three visiting surgeons and three visiting physicians in 1770. The number had risen to five of each class by 1802, but was reduced once more to three of each in the reforms of that year. They included Sir Isaac Pennington, Regius Professor of Physic, Sir Busick Harwood, Professor of Anatomy, and T. V. Okes, whose pamphlet on the Cambridge epidemic of 1815 has been quoted above. By the end of the 19th century the visiting staff had risen to eleven, and the resident staff to four. The matron, besides a domestic staff of 21, had some 40 nurses and probationers working under her, for in 1877 a training school for nurses had been established by Alice Fisher, the matron.

Adden brooke's had been serving as a medical school ever since 1841 when the governors had made regulations for the admission of students. The report for 1889 describes it as a large and important medical school, recognized both by the University and the examining bodies as a place of training, and arrangements were being made with the University for lectures to be given there by persons who were not members of the hospital staff. In 1900, by an arrangement with the University, the Regius Professor of Physic and the Professor of Surgery were elected as additional members of the medical staff. New arrangements had to be made for the teaching of students from October 1936 owing to changes in the curriculum. Addenbrooke's is recognized by the University as a place of clinical study.

Since 1948 the whole organization of the hospital has become part of the National Health Service, and Addenbrooke's forms one of the group of United Cambridge Hospitals which supply the principal hospital service for the eastern counties. The other members of the group are the Chesterton Hospital in Union Lane, Brookfield Hospital in Mabel Lane, and the Cambridge Maternity Hospital in Mill Road, formerly the poor law infirmary. The joint medical staff in 1950 numbered 46.

Growth of The City

Cambridge is essentially a town that has originated from the two bridgeheads that guarded the crossing of the Cam by the Roman Road the Hadstock or Huntingdon Way of the Middle Ages: what has recently been described as the 'spine' of the town. The ground plan of its nucleus is based on the junction with this road, just south of the bridge, of the road coming north from Trumpington the High Street of the Middle Ages. The position of the earliest settlements was determined by the gravel ridge where dwellings were above flood level. The names Peas hill and Market hill today preserve the tradition of an elevation now obliterated, whilst north of the river the Roman camp was planted on the one high spot where the chalk outlier rose to over 70 ft.

It has been suggested by Arthur Gray that the waters of the Cam were artificially directed to serve as outworks to the north and south of the river crossing at a period when Middle Anglians and East Anglians were contending for mastery, and the further hypothesis that the King's Ditch was the outer line, and possibly the last of a series of ditches constructed to defend the crossing, may well be valid. The line of the ditch is best seen on a map; the two 'gates', probably toll barriers, were Barnwell Gate, where the Hadstock Way crossed the ditch, hard by the present site of Christ's College, and Trumpington Gate, where the High Street crossed it, at the top of Mill Lane.

Archaeological evidence indicates early postRoman settlement on the market site, and probably there was a substantial settlement round the market and St. Bene't's Church well before 1066. The green belt separating the two centres of population is, as Gray showed, easily traceable down to 1279. The alluvial strip was not suitable for buildings until it had been raised by the accumulated deposits of centuries. If we judge by the churches, of which St. Clement, St. George, St. Michael, St. Edward, St. Botolph, and St. Peter were probably there by the end of the 11th century, the line of the medieval High Street was preferred to the Hadstock Way, later known as Conduit Street inside the ditch and Preachers' Street outside it, and today represented by Sidney Street and Regent Street. It was in the 13th century that the made land between the High Street and the river began to be built on. Milne Street, running through the parish of St. John Zachary, contained many dwelling houses later to be replaced by religious houses and University hostels. In the 12th century St. John's Hospital had been erected on a 'very poor waste place'.

Apart from the houses within the King's Ditch, the settlement round Barnwell Abbey, whither the Austin canons moved in 1112, is on land inhabited in pagan Anglo-Saxon times, and there is evidence of an equally ancient origin for the little settlement at Newnham. St. Radegund's nunnery was also outside the ditch, and in the 13th century the Dominicans' house was outside the Barnwell Gate, as St. Peter's Church and College were outside the Trumpington Gate. Thus apart from the old castle end, there were four suburbs to the east and south when the survey of 1279 was made.

Maitland has familiarized us with the picture of the small urban nucleus of medieval Cambridge surrounded by the open fields so beautifully depicted by Loggan in 1690 lying in the form of threequarters of a rough circle, of which the fourth quarter is made up of the vill of Chesterton, only to be added to the others in 1912. If the circle was ever complete, it may be that the Chesterton segment was subtracted when William I built his castle on the site of the Roman camp and made it the governmental centre of Cambridgeshire. Chesterton was one of the very few royal manors in the county. However that may be, the proportion of open arable to built-up area was something like 23 to 9 until the end of the 18th century.

The survey of 1279 fills 45 closely printed pages of the *Rotuli Hundredorum*, as against the half page that Domesday Book allots to Cambridge. It enumerates, parish by parish, every house, shop, and void place in the borough. In 1279 there were 3 parishes north of the river and 14 south. There were 17 churches, not counting those of the religious houses, but as yet no college. There were 76 shops or stalls, 48 of them in the parishes of St. Edward and St. Mary by the Market. There were 5 granges, 6 granaries, 3 water-mills, 2 windmills, and 2 horsemills. There were 535 messuages, and the householder of every one is named, with the rent that he paid to his landlord, if he had one, and the dues that he paid to the town bailiffs if his house was rated to the hawgavel and so contributed to the fee farm.

Since the amount paid in hawgavel in 1279 was practically unchanged since 1086, this evidence gives a valuable clue as to the location of dwellings at these two dates. In the Castle End there were 73 houses in 1279, 22 of which paid hawgavel and were, therefore, presumably, on sites inhabited in 1086. In the parishes of St. Mary the Great, St. Bene't, St. Edward, and St. Botolph, the region round the market, there were 159 houses and 59 shops: of these 63 holdings paid hawgavel. In St. Clement's parish there were 40 dwellings of which 15 paid hawgavel; in St. Sepulchre's and All Saints' parishes only 3 out of 22 paid it. Outside the ditch, in the Barnwell suburb, there were 95 houses, only 20 of which paid hawgavel. Outside Barnwell Gate, there were 12 houses of which 2 were liable; outside Trumpington Gate, there were 28, of which 3 were liable, and across the river at Newnham 20 houses, of which 1 only was liable. Besides this suburban growth, a new quarter of the town had come into existence within the ditch, between the High Street and the river. Milne Street ran through it parallel with the High Street, and it was served by St. John Zachary. Along the river a row of hithes had grown up between the Great Bridge and the mills. The concentration of the Jews in the parts opposite St. John's hospital had given the name of the Jewry to the neighbourhood of All Saints' and St. Sepulchre's churches, and the name of *Vicus Judeorum* to what is now All Saints' passage.

The survey, as we have seen, indicates the existence of four suburbs. A careful study of two of them about this time has been made by H. P. Stokes. His map of Cambridge outside Trumpington Gate in 1270 shows the ribbon development either side of the road after it has crossed the King's Ditch into the Eastern Fields. There are five University hostels, two on the site soon to be occupied by Peterhouse, and two on the other side of the road where Pembroke was to rise in the 14th century. Besides several smaller houses, those of three wealthy burgess families of Cambridge are traceable, whose names occur on the list of the Mayors and bailiffs of Henry III's reign. The Ailsham house was to pass to Peterhouse; the Le Rus house with its Chapel of St. Lucy had been acquired by the Friars of the Sack in 1258, and the St. Edmund's house, with the chapel whose dedication had given its name to the family, was to be occupied by the Canons of Sempringham in 1291.

Outside the Barnwell Gate, St. Andrew's Church may go back to Saxon days, but it is first mentioned by name in 1200, and the Dominican Friars' house, the forerunner of Emmanuel College, was building in 1238. The survey of 1279 expressly states that there were several private houses on the site before the friars came, but there is little information about them; the suburb cannot have been so popular for residence as that near St. Peter's Church. Two University hostels were located along the road. On the west side, well beyond Langrith Lane, was Rudd's, first mentioned in 1283. It later became the Castle Inn. On the east side stood St. Nicholas, first mentioned in 1393.

No such details are available about the much more populous suburb that stretched out along the Newmarket Road towards Barnwell, nor do the maps of the 16th century onward extend so far.

The 14th-century subsidy rolls give some indication of the growth of the town a generation later. The taxpayers of the tallage of 1304 are listed by parishes, and the outstanding feature of the list is the filling up of the green belt. The four parishes round the market with Holy Trinity contained 234 taxpayers, the three parishes in Castle End, 49. The parishes of St. Clement, St. Sepulchre, and All Saints in the Jewry, however, contained 135, whereas in 1279 there had only been 62 houses in that area.

The returns for the fifteenth of 1314–15 are by wards. The ward beyond the bridge contained 40 taxpayers; the Heyward, along

Hadstock Way, 50; Trumpington Ward along the High Street, 98; Market Ward, 122; Milne Street Ward with Newnham, 65; Barnwell Ward, 29; and the ward this side the bridge, 65. And whereas the average rate of tax due was 2s. 1d. a head in the less eligible Trumpington Ward, and was 2s. 11d. in the prosperous Market Ward, it was 3s. 4d. in the ward this side the bridge. Here wealthy newcomers like Roger of Harleston built their houses. The green belt of 1279 was the fashionable quarter of 1314. On the other hand, there were some large private houses with gardens in the region between Milne Street and High Street where Gonville Hall and Trinity Hall, King's Hall and Michaelhouse were to be built. Some belonged to churchmen like the Prior of Ely, and some to laymen like Niel of Thornton, Simon de Brune, or Sir John of Cambridge.

As has been seen there is evidence of stagnation, if not retrogression, in the 14th and 15th centuries. The colleges and University hostels were taking up more and more of the space between the High Street and the river. The building of King's College cut Milne Street in half, but Henry VI provided Garret Hostel Lane as an alternative. Salthithe also disappeared, and the Church of St. John Zachary shared the fate of All Saints by the Castle, which had been closed after the Black Death. A large vacant space, tenanted by bleating sheep, awaited for many years the building of Henry's College. In 1446 the town bewailed the loss of population and trade resulting from the encroachments of the colleges; but in the multiplication of vacant places it was sharing the lot of many other 15th-century towns.

With Lyne's map of 1574 we reach a cartographical picture, but one that does not extend to Barnwell. All the colleges are there, except Emmanuel, Sidney Sussex, and Downing. Houses are thickest along the 'spine' and along the road ascending Castle Hill as far as the empty churchyard of All Saints. But behind the street frontage there are unoccupied spaces on Pound Hill, and between Preachers' Street and the High Street, where there is a large garden area. The site of the Grey Friars is almost empty, there are no houses along Walls Lane and the slopes below the castle are unoccupied. The ditch has been covered over in Mill Lane, but is open all the rest of its course. The School of Pythagoras is to be seen beyond the river.

Hamond's magnificent map of 1592 is the basis for most of our detailed knowledge of the town layout for earlier as well as Elizabethan times; in especial for the market area. Most of the hithes along the Cam have disappeared. The open spaces are being encroached upon; tenements are being added as well as subdivided, which gives point to the complaints of the University and the exhortations of the Privy Council. Houses are appearing on the castle slopes and the space behind Magdalene College is losing much of its garden ground. But outside the ditch future compensation was to be secured twenty years later, when, in 1613, the town acquired, in exchange for Garrett Hostel Green west of the Cam, the 25 acres which had in 1587 been leased by Trinity College to Edward Parker, the college cook. Parker's Piece, later the scene of feasts and parliamentary elections, is one of the finest open spaces of any town in England. The map of 1634 shows Perse's Grammar School in what is now Free School Lane, Hobson's Workhouse, and his conduit in Trumpington Street. There is now a continuous row of houses along both sides of Walls Lane, where the ditch is crossed by many little footbridges.

Loggan in 1688 shows in the north the Cromwellian earthworks on Castle Hill, and in the south Pembroke Piece. The space between Bridge Street and Trinity Street has become the congested mass of small courts condemned by the health inspector in 1849; a condition practically identical with that shown a hundred years later in Custance's map of 1798. No trace of the former wide garden space with trees remains; even the name of Green Street is taken from Oliver Green. By 1798 there is no room left within the ditch; there is a crop of houses all along Walls Lane to the Newmarket Road, but otherwise there are fewer differences than might have been expected. All the evidence goes to show that the four suburbs of 1279 had hardly increased their built-up area when the Inclosure Acts of 1801 and 1807 came to permit of natural expansion.

The map of Cambridge in 1830 shows the first fruits of inclosure. Downing College is in occupation, to the south, of St. Thomas' Leys and the Marsh where Gunning remembered gownsmen shooting snipe. Houses are to be seen along the Newmarket Road beyond Jesus, and along the Huntingdon Road beyond the Castle. But these were merely beginnings.

Between 1801 and 1841 the population of the parish of St. Andrew the Less, Barnwell, had risen from 252 to 9,486; more than the whole population of Cambridge in 1801. A new town had sprung up between Parker's Piece and Barnwell. The names of the streets in this area give the date of origin: Fitzroy, the family name of Lord Euston, University burgess 1784–1811; Burleigh, the Cambridge carrier who furnished horses and wagons for military service in 1798. The other great extension was to the south of Parker's Piece.

By 1851 the movement out of the centre was becoming marked; the courtyards were being opened up and the fire in the market-place gave an opportunity for further clearance. Many families were removing to the neighbouring suburb of Chesterton, where, according to the census returns, 200 new houses had been built in the last ten years. In the second half of the 19th century the chief extension was westwards over Newnham and southwards towards Cherry Hinton and Trumpington. The expansion northwards towards Milton and north-west along the Huntingdon Road did not come until the 20th century, and Girton was still isolated by a wide belt of arable land when Emily Davies planted her College there in 1873, at the far end of what was once the hamlet called Howes.

The End

www.ingramcontent.com/pod-product-compliance
Lightning Source LLC
Chambersburg PA
CBHW031104080526
44587CB00011B/812